LIVING WELL

LIVING WELL

The New York Times

BOOK OF HOME DESIGN AND DECORATION
EDITED BY CARRIE DONOVAN

BOOK DESIGN BY MICHAEL VALENTI

Times
BOOKS

Published by TIMES BOOKS, a division
of Quadrangle/The New York Times Book Co., Inc.
Three Park Avenue, New York, N.Y. 10016

Published simultaneously in Canada by
Fitzhenry & Whiteside, Ltd., Toronto

Library of Congress Cataloging in Publication Data
Main entry under title:

Living well.

1. Interior decoration.   I.Donovan, Carrie.   II.
The New York Times.
NK2130. L65   729   81-50088
ISBN   0-8129-0993-3   AACR2.

Printed in the U.S.A.

LIVING WELL
ACKNOWLEDGMENTS

This book exists because *The New York Times* exists. It is an institution that demands — and receives — thought-provoking yet responsible reporting on every subject. *Living Well* is dedicated to this fine institution and its excellent editors, critics, reporters, and contributors.

A great debt of gratitude is due Robert McDonald for his cogent thinking and concise sizing-up of all sorts of things, including the title — and to Edward Klein for his succinct editing of the latter. Alison MacFarlane's intelligence and cool competence, not to mention mellifluous voice, kept this whole project going. Melanie Fleischmann was a polite but relentless pursuer of photographers and elusive personalities. Michael Valenti, with Diana LaGuardia assisting, not only turned out handsome, distinguished layouts, but turned the magazine's art department into a home-away-from-home for nights and weekends on end. (A vote of thanks to Al's Delicatessen, too, for the egg salad sandwiches which sustained all through same.)

The Marilyns — Bethany and Pelo, Suzanne Slesin, Ruth Ansel, and Ann Schumacher were all sympathetic sounding boards. From Paris, Josette Lazar, and from London, Heather Bradley, lent helping hands. Leonard Schwartz, Patrick Filley, and Hugh Howard of Times Books; Bill Young and Jed Stevenson's technical know-how, Jack Palmer's lab work; Jack Hallihan's fleet feet; Susan Smahl Plummer's telephone expertise; and Helena Gillen's patient picking up after us — all helped to make this book possible.

INTRODUCTION

It is a question of mind over matter. One can live well almost anywhere — on top of a mountain, or in the valley below; high in a skyscraper, or burrowed in the earth; more outdoors than in, or just the reverse; in a climate that is hot, temperate, or cold, or each of those in turn; in the East, the North, the West, or the South; in one room or many; in a palazzo, a villa, a sprawling country house, a compact condominium, or even a simple shelter.

The logistics and locations for habitable space are many indeed. But if a space is a place in which to live well, certain things have happened to it. First and foremost, a point of view has been imposed by the inhabitants, present or past, or perhaps by the architect or designer who originally conceived it. Also, one should sense a definite personality about the place — one that hopefully reflects the current occupant — for the place or places we call home should be our own. Finally, the space should be as comfortable as possible to truly cosset all who live or visit there.

No question about it, money helps. It takes plenty to recruit the services of the best craftsmen and planners, architects and interior designers and decorators. And plenty more to acquire the best to fill a space. But sometimes imagination and ingenuity can tilt the tables toward accomplishing the best living space, too.

This book is a collection of some noteworthy spaces that have been singled out by *The New York Times'* editors, critics, reporters, and contributors. They range everywhere from a magnificent palazzo set in the hills overlooking Genoa, Italy to a redesigned New York City tenement to a designer's cozy country retreat in France to a fixed-up camper for a two-person, five-dog American family. But they all have one thing in common: They are all eminently equipped for living well.

— **Carrie Donovan**

IN A KITCHEN

This is the heart of the house. Long since promoted from a room dedicated to the preparation of food and the requisite before and after drudgery, the kitchen has become the center of everything: It is a place in which to entertain, eat, watch television, supervise children, write, meditate, and raise the roof, as well as, of course, to cook and clean up. In short, the kitchen is a place in which to live. To many, it is a space so important that it warrants the investment of time and money and the special attention of the best architects, interior designers, or decorators.

This superb modern kitchen, designed jointly by the owner and the architect, Alan Buchsbaum, is outfitted with the best appliances, including a restaurant stove with a gleaming backsplash.

HIGH-TECH GLAMOUR

THE
INDUSTRIAL
STYLE OF
DÉCOR
IS GIVEN A
TOUCH
OF LUXURY.

The familiar elements of the high-tech style are present in force — glass-block windows, restaurant stove, industrial lamps, coffee-shop shelving, plenty of stainless steel. Yet this kitchen is not high tech as we have known it. Gone is the no-nonsense functionalism. Absent, too, are many of the economies that made high tech so accessible. What remains is the fundamental soundness of the design, but glamorized.

Or, as the owner, Roseann Hirsch, aptly put it, "This is not high tech; this is high maintenance." "I think the kitchen is attractive, but I wouldn't want to have to keep it clean," agreed the architect Alan Buchsbaum, who, with his associate German Martinez, helped the Hirsches with the design. But, Mrs. Hirsch said, "If the look is right, I don't care what else I have to sacrifice."

And, as it happens, the look is dazzling. Unexpected materials warm the steel and tile iciness. The tiles are the rough, Mexican type. Mirror backsplashes lift coffee-shop shelving to elegance. Bentwood chairs and a long, wood table give the dining area a note of well-worn warmth.

Bright touches of brass abound and, as a result, such normally unnotable elements as the brass locks on the standard steel fire door become points in the décor.

— BY MARILYN BETHANY

LEFT: *An unexpected mix of materials imbues the kitchen with its own brand of charm.*

RIGHT, ABOVE: *The mirrored backsplashes provide the room with additional touches of flash.*

RIGHT, BELOW: *The dining area is made warm and livable by well-worn wood furnishings.*

THE LIVE-IN KITCHEN

A SPACE FOR LIVING AND ENTERTAINING AS WELL AS FOR COOKING AND EATING

This is a kitchen that seems to accept the inevitable: It has a living room built in. It is, in truth, a space for living and entertaining as well as cooking and eating. The designer, Tom O'Toole, envisioned a flexible space that not only combines formality and informality, but would be a logical center for many activities — as kitchens often are.

On the kitchen side, a chest-high island containing a range, a sink, cabinets, and counter space is angled into the room, making it accessible but separate. It is flanked by more counter space, another sink, a refrigerator, and a wall of gray, stained-oak cabinets.

The living side of the room has a banquette and a round dining table, plus sofas and chairs that are easily moved to adapt the room to a variety of uses — dining, TV-watching, games, or just conversation. The walls are painted a glowing coral and the floor is covered with white ceramic tile with two colored borders.
— **BY GEORGE O'BRIEN**

ABOVE: *The living area of this combined kitchen and family room has sofas and chairs that can be moved to serve a variety of activities.*

RIGHT: *The cooking area, with ample storage and counter space, was placed at an accessible angle to the room.*

16

IN A BEDROOM

Essentially meant for sleeping, the well-worked-out bedroom supplies the solutions to all sorts of other situations as well. Primarily, it should be a "withdrawing" room — a place for privacy, for cosseting the occupants with as many or as few amenities as they feel they need. It can be large or small; the actual square footage allotted is not nearly as important as the ambience that is created.

This bedroom, designed by John Saladino, achieves its romantic aura through mauve-toned walls and the glow of the fire within the marble Georgian fireplace. The bed, covered with quilted aubergine silk, seems to float in the middle of this serene retreat.

FRESH DRESSING

TRADITIONAL SETTINGS ARE GIVEN A NEW, WARM APPEAL.

"The light quality in a room is the thing I start with," said designer Katherine Stephens. To capture the sun in this room with a southern exposure, she painted the ceilings yellow to insure year-round sunlight and added luminescent chintz draperies.

The room's furnishings are a mixture of periods and styles; what pulls them together is their quality. "I tried to choose things for the room that would be both collectible and useful," she said.

Designer Susan Zises decided to turn the tiny space below into an apartment bedroom, "one in which anyone would be comfortable, from a young woman to a dowager, but also one which would be inviting for a man to be in." The plaid balloon shades hide the elevator shaft the room overlooks. The built-in bed alcove is made of plywood upholstered in white cotton quilting material. The alcove is draped with several layers of sheer organdy with pinked edges for a feminine look.

RIGHT: *The natural light in this room is intensified by its yellow ceiling and fresh colorings.*

BELOW: *A purple chair, echoed in lavender sheets, is an unexpected swath of color in this small room.*

PHOTOGRAPHS BY RALPH BOGERTMAN

20

IN A BATHROOM

Certainly, no home is complete without at least one. And, like the kitchen, the bathroom is currently being given the professional treatment. Gone is the notion of it simply as a place to take care of the bare essentials as privately as possible. The bathroom is now viewed as a closet, a spa, a gymnasium, or even a family room.

The components of this black and chrome bathroom-turned-spa created by Eric Bernard Designs include a weight- *training machine, a home-viewing computer, and a revolving clothes rack.*

22

COMPUTERIZED DRAMA

The components of this private retreat read like an electrical catalog. Neatly worked into this luxurious room are an exercising machine, a hydro-massage tub, a steam machine, a revolving clothes rack (such as those at the dry cleaners), an upholstered, multi-positional gray, chaise longue, a home computer with its viewing screen, a stereo sound system, and a track lighting system that allows for thirty different lighting effects. The two-way mirrors on the closet doors and over the built-in combination dressing table and desk turn transparent when lighted from behind. The entire room — floors, walls, and ceiling — is covered with Italian ceramic tiles colored a low luster satin black that gives a visual impression of leather. Chrome-plated metal structural details add a note of shimmering drama. The room was created by Eric Bernard Designs.

— BY GEORGE O'BRIEN

LEFT: *A custom-designed stereo sound system is built into one wall of this black-tiled exercise-relaxation-dressing room.*
TOP: *The electrically operated chaise longue, covered in handwoven cotton chenille,* has an almost limitless range of positions.
ABOVE: *The glass-enclosed hydro-massage tub has vents in the ceiling that eject steam into the enclosure from a machine located under the chaise.*

OPEN-ENDED BATHROOMS

THE LATEST BATHROOMS ARE AS WHOLESOME AS OUTDOORS.

When the history of American interior design is written, the 70's will surely be remembered as the Epoch of the Palazzo Bath. During that so-called me-generation decade, scrubbing among the swells was commonly performed in surroundings that rivaled for unbridled opulence a flamboyant Hollywood set designer's meditations on Imperial Rome.

Then, a new style of bathroom began to emerge and, while it may not be for everyone, it is as long on back-to-nature beauty as its predecessor was on artifice. These bathrooms are surfaced with such wholesome materials as natural wood, ceramic tile, and Sheetrock — simple, straightforward, clean-cut. Unlike palazzo baths, whose glamour seldom had any stylistic connection with the rest of a house, the new bathroom is meant to blend seamlessly with adjacent rooms — so seamlessly, in fact, that it may not even attempt to gain full status as a separate space. Often, doors are eliminated entirely and walls do not necessarily extend full height from the floor to the ceiling. These bathrooms open onto bedrooms which, themselves, may be open to the rest of the house. The bathroom, that last bastion of total privacy, has fallen prey to togetherness.

"Bathroom habits are not necessarily something to be either hidden or glorified," said Peter Shelton, of the firm Shelton, Stortz, Mindel and Associates, who designed the room at right. Like all proponents of shared-experience bathing, Shelton believes that the daily toilette is necessary, natural, and so should be treated with realistic nonchalance.

"There are levels of privacy," Shelton explained. "In this bathroom, there is a zone of total privacy — a toilet stall with its own sink. Then there is a bath area that is partially open to the bedroom. Here the user is revealed to a point. And the bedroom can either open to the rest of the apartment or be closed off with a sliding door. Frankly, I get lonely in a closed-off bath."

In an open-plan bathroom designed by Michael Rubin and Henry Smith-Miller, eschewing privacy was the client's idea. In their original drawings, the architects had specified that an opening between the second-floor bathroom and an adjacent, double-height, ground-floor room should be filled with glass. "The bathroom needed light and a sense of expanded space, so we didn't want to do a solid wall," Rubin said. "But, before the glass could be installed, the client decided that it wasn't needed because no one could see into the room."

Fine, perhaps, for family, but how do guests respond to all this openness? Said Dale Slomoff, a photographer's representative who recently took over a friend's one-room apartment, complete with semiopen bath, "When I used to visit here, I'd wonder, 'How could anyone live like this?'" But despite his initial misgivings, he has learned to love the place. "I've gotten used to it," Slomoff said. "And friends don't seem to mind it much."

— BY MARILYN BETHANY

TOP: *This bathroom is open to an adjacent room to take advantage of the natural light.*
ABOVE: *The architects originally intended to fill the* gap *between the second-floor bathroom and an adjacent, double-height ground-floor room with glass, but the client felt it unnecessary.*

Levels of privacy: A bathroom, which is open to the master bedroom, separated only by the free-standing mirror, has a stall (not shown) containing the toilet and sink that can be closed off with a door.

PHOTOGRAPHS BY GENE MAGGIO/THE NEW YORK TIMES

BATHING IN THE OPEN

THE TUB IS TREATED AS THOUGH IT WERE A SOFA IN A SALON.

Once hidden behind locked doors, the bath and shower have come out in the open, merging with the bedroom to form a bath/dressing/exercise complex.

Robert Mihalik, a sculptor who is also a free-lance designer and a fabricator of custom cabinetry, devoted roughly one-fourth of his 2,400-square-foot loft in SoHo to a bath complex that includes a soaking tub and exercise area. "Some people prefer to spend $20,000 on sofas and furniture or on a gourmet kitchen," he said. "I felt that the bath outweighed those other priorities."

A shower is behind the tub and can be opened or closed from view by a mirrored sliding panel.

Alan Buchsbaum, an architect with Design Coalition, distinctly remembers his first encounter with the soaking tub when he spent time in Japan. That design feature has shown up in many bathrooms designed by Mr. Buchsbaum.

One that he recently completed has a recessed whirlpool tub set in a tiled platform several steps up from the bed area. Mr. Buchsbaum designed the soaking tub, which seats three comfortably, in a free-form shape. Its companion shower is not curtained.

"The rationale seems to be that if you're friendly enough to live with somebody," Mr. Buchsbaum said, "then it's not too farfetched to bathe in front of them."

— BY NORMA SKURKA

LEFT: *The redwood hot tub in Robert Mihalik's loft is flush with the floor — a step up from the platform holding his bed. Two steps down is an exercise area. A sliding mirror closes off the shower and hides storage space.*

ABOVE: *Alan Buchsbaum, the architect, put bath and shower on a tiled platform beneath an existing loft skylight. The plants and chair do not have to be removed for bathing.*

AS THE DESIGNERS DO

Creative people do not usually reside, much less thrive, in mundane environments, especially after they achieve some amount of success. Their instinctive need for expressing their talents spills over into all facets of their lives, including, of course, where and how they live. Though their points of view often vary widely — even among those who toil in the same field of endeavor — in this instance, fashion — the results are invariably fascinating, often unusual, almost always handsome and elegant and unfailingly revealing of the personality that lives within.

The private entrance hall to designer Karl Lagerfeld's Paris home in the wing of a splendid eighteenth-century house has a sweeping sandstone staircase with a filigree, wrought-iron railing. The floor is checkered marble. A formal floral arrangement always nests in a niche near the outside door.

PHOTOGRAPHS BY SERGE KORNILOFF

KARL'S CASTLE

A PARIS HOME IN A WING OF AN EIGHTEENTH-CENTURY HOUSE

Karl Lagerfeld's taste has taken many turns in the last ten years. These shifts have shown up in the designer's fashion designs for Chloé and in the way he has chosen to live — always on the move.

Until 1977, he lived in a high-ceilinged apartment surrounded by priceless Art Deco objects and furniture. Then, he suddenly sold everything at auction and moved into a new home — just as everyone else in Paris was discovering, and buying, Art Deco. "I have always loved the Art Deco period," said Karl, "but my first, and constant, love has been the French eighteenth century. I studied the architecture of that period and have been collecting its furniture for years."

TOP: *The tapestries of Karl Lagerfeld's eighteenth-century daybed depict the four seasons. The bed stands in a room where the ceiling frescoes depict the same theme.*
ABOVE: *The exterior of the house, like the interior, is* *formal, with an archway opening onto a central courtyard.*
RIGHT: *A small salon of elegant carved wood paneling has a marble fireplace and is furnished with simple period pieces and garnet silk moiré curtains.*

It is in this style that he is furnishing his new home — which is, appropriately, one wing of an eighteenth-century Paris house. Its rooms are sumptuous and, although Karl Lagerfeld has not used much furniture, the effect is elegant. "People never did put much furniture into rooms at that time. It was later, in the nineteenth century, that the pompous furnishing, the bourgeois filling of large rooms started. I live here the same way they did. Dinners by fire and candle-light." But not in a dining room. That also, according to Karl, was an invention of the bourgeoisie.

"At Versailles, for example, tables were set up anywhere, according to the number of people to be served. Here, I have food kept hot at one central table and people are able to move from room to room pulling up chairs to big, simple tables covered in long white cloth. It is a casual life in a sumptuous setting."

— BY MARY RUSSELL

LEFT: *One of the entrance salons with a delicate, small white velvet couch.*

TOP: *M. Lagerfeld's bedroom has a canopied bed in original eighteenth-century flowered silk.*

CENTER, LEFT: *The view from the top of the entrance stairway.*

CENTER, RIGHT: *A ceiling motif in the main salon.*

RIGHT: *The designer's glasses rest on an eighteenth-century side table.*

FAR RIGHT: *The ultramodern, functional mirror and chrome master bathroom. This and the kitchen are the only twentieth-century rooms in the house.*

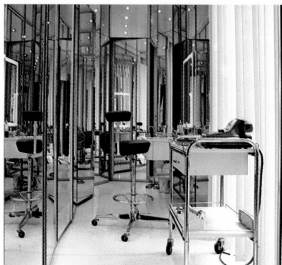

HALSTON'S HIDEAWAY

SIMPLE ELEMENTS ARRANGED IN PERFECT COMPOSITION.

The fashion designer Halston's house, built by the well-known architect Paul Rudolph on Manhattan's East Side in 1967 for a real-estate lawyer, is spare but totally luxurious. Standing inside it, one cannot help but think of Halston's own designs, since the ideas that underlie the architecture parallel the designer's own themes: simple elements arranged in perfect composition, with the feeling of lushness coming not from excess activity but from elegant materials and a superb sense of balance.

"I know this house was designed for somebody else," Halston said. "But I really feel as though it was built for me."

Technically, the house is a remodeling of a carriage house, but Rudolph's renovation was so total that it is, for all practical purposes, a new building. It is at its most spectacular within, but the facade is every bit as remarkable. It is a subtle composition of steel and dark glass, with a gently projecting upper floor as a cornicelike horizontal element, a strong vertical center, and a solid base. The facade reflects interior functions perfectly, yet it works equally well as a composition in its own right.

The dark glass, for all its sobriety, suggests that there is great drama going on inside, and indeed there is. A narrow hall, with white walls and floors of slate, leads back to the heart of the house, where the space suddenly expands to a vast living room, twenty-

seven feet high, backed by a three-story greenhouse and surrounded by balconies, open stairs, and platforms, each of which functions as a place floating at a precise point in space. It is a remarkable space indeed, large yet intimate, active yet serene. There are many things going on — stairs running up the side, light coming in from skylights and the greenhouse, changes in level — yet one never feels buffeted by all the activity. The house manages an almost perfect balance between forcing itself upon us and leaving us alone.

Halston has renovated his home somewhat, and his efforts have mostly been along the lines of simplification. "I like it white and sparse," he said. "I wanted to take out some things that were just decorative." Out, therefore, went an enormous bookcase and some sculpture on a sit-

TOP: *The fashion designer Halston.*

LEFT: *Floating planes characterize the living-room stairs and balcony sitting area. The furniture was designed by architect Paul Rudolph.*

ABOVE: *The facade is a diagram of dark glass.*

PHOTOGRAPHS BY HIRO

37

UPSTAIRS, THE HOUSE HAS AN INTRICATE ARRANGEMENT OF ROOMS.

ting-room balcony; the too lush tropical greenhouse was reworked by Robert Lester into a simple and extraordinarily elegant bamboo forest; and the art on the walls was reduced to a minimum. (In some cases, the art is literally minimal — there is a blank canvas by Victor Hugo intended not as a work of art but as a device to give a huge wall in the living room a bit of texture.)

"At first you want to change everything when you move into a house like this," Halston said. "But the house is such a work of art you end up giving in to it."

The house has an intricate arrangement of rooms upstairs. A master-bedroom suite is one level above the living room; its sitting area overlooks the living room as an open balcony, while the bedroom itself rises two stories along the front of the house. The bedroom is enclosed and private, although it is in the front, and it points up an important aspect of the house's design: The enclosed spaces are in the front, to act as a wall to the street, whereas the open areas are in the rear.

At the back of the living room, one level higher than the master bedroom, another balcony serves as a guest room or study. The top, or fourth, floor contains a bedroom, living room, and small kitchen, which can function as a separate apartment.

— BY PAUL GOLDBERGER

ABOVE: *Halston's bedroom is one and a half stories high and epitomizes the cool, restrained elegance of the rest of the house.*

LEFT: *The top-floor sitting room, the most conventional part of the house, is made distinctive by Andy Warhol's portrait of Halston. This top-floor suite opens onto a roof garden; it can also be used as a separate apartment.*

RIGHT: *The living room of Halston's house is spare and elegant, a careful composition highlighted by a bamboo forest.*

38

PALOMA'S
NEST, I

A DESIGNER SET OFF HER FIRST TURN-OF-THE-CENTURY INTERIOR WITH ART DECO FURNISHINGS.

Paloma Picasso, the daughter of the artist Pablo Picasso, has had two uniquely beautiful apartments in Paris. This is the first.

"I love living in hotels," said Paloma Picasso. We were sitting in the drawing room of her apartment near the Seine. The building is sturdy 1900s bourgeois — high ceilings, delicate wall moldings, arched windows, arched mirrors over carved marble fireplaces, shiny wood floors, lots of windows, and lots of light.

The walls of the salon and adjoining rooms are pink — a soft flattering pink. "To give a good complexion," said Mlle. Picasso. There are no curtains on the windows that stretch from floor to ceiling. This was deliberate. "The wooden frames and brass knobs are so beautiful."

There is a bit of a hotel feeling in the apartment. The living room could be compared with a reception salon in a luxurious turn-of-the-

LEFT: *Pink pervades Paloma Picasso's first apartment. In the salon, pink walls and carpet set off an aquamarine satin sofa and chairs by Art Deco designer Groult. The painting was a wedding present from Andy Warhol.*

ABOVE: *Paloma Picasso in the drawing room of the apartment.*

41

century palace. People come and go, for the apartment contains the working studios as well as the living quarters of Mlle. Picasso and her husband, Argentine playwright and director Rafael López Sanchez.

Mlle. Picasso, who loves furniture from the 1920s and 30s, avidly attends auctions and haunts her favorite antique shops looking for finds like the plaster "palm tree" floor lamps designed by Serge Roche.

In the oval dining room are six straight-backed oak chairs, signed by the Art Deco designer Ruhlmann. In one corner is Mlle. Picasso's special treasure, a Persian chest of ebony inlaid with mother-of-pearl. It is, she said, "the only piece of furniture I have from my childhood and my parents' home in Vallauris."

"The important thing," she said, "is space to do everything we like."

— BY MARY RUSSELL

LEFT: *A cool atrium room filled with white wicker furniture and open to the balcony.*

TOP: *In a corner of the salon, a Deco chrome and glass cocktail cart.*

ABOVE, LEFT: *Mlle. Picasso's special treasure is this Persian chest of ebony inlaid with mother-of-pearl. It comes from her parents' house in Vallauris, where she spent her childhood.*

ABOVE, RIGHT: *In the dining room, windows are left bare to show off the beauty of their arches and moldings. On the wall, a tiny portrait of Mlle. Picasso done by her father, Pablo Picasso, when she was four years old.*

PALOMA'S NEST, II

THE CURRENT HOME OF THE PARIS-BASED DESIGNER

The apartment I had before, my first real apartment, was like a big hotel in the south of France — grand, but not too comfortable. I think lost space, rooms you never enter, protect you from the world," said Paloma Picasso.

"We were looking for a complete change in where we lived," continued Mlle. Picasso, a jewelry designer who, as Mme. Picasso López, is married to Rafael López Sanchez, the Argentine playwright and director. "We wanted a duplex, a view, a terrace, or a garden."

A two-year search ended with the discovery of a charming ("or at least we knew it would be when we finished …") ground-floor garden apartment in a prerevolutionary building on the Left Bank, a short stroll from St. Germain-des-Prés.

Not only were the rooms gracefully proportioned, flooded with sunlight, and rich in architectural detail — featuring superb moldings, mirrors, and niches — but they could park their car in the cobblestone courtyard. Thus Mlle. Picasso, undeterred by the fact that she could negotiate only a three-year lease, set to work realizing every ounce of the potential she envisioned for their six-room prize.

"This time I started with fabric — a stripe," she said, "and the stripe just kept on going." Commencing with a delicate apricot-and-cream striped moiré at the soaring French windows, the stripe theme continues throughout an off-white living room where moldings are highlighted in shimmering gold and relief panels accented by

ABOVE: *Paloma Picasso and her husband, Rafael López Sanchez, in the living room of their Paris apartment.*

RIGHT: *The off-white living room with moldings highlighted in gold and relief panels accented in a surprising creamy cerise. The upholstered chairs are by André Groult, the 1930s artist.*

a surprising creamy cerise. "I call it raspberries-mashed-with-milk," observed the designer.

Mlle. Picasso has carried her theme of stripes to her dining room with a yellow-and-white pavilion fabric on the walls and a matching bouffant Austrian shade on a large window.

By and large the furniture in the apartment, some of which was used in her former apartment, was designed in the 1930s by artists whose works have recently come to be much sought after by collectors. The upholstered chairs in the living room, for instance, were made by André Groult while Jean Michel Frank was responsible for the pair of parchment-covered coffee tables. In the dining room there is a set of chairs by E. J. Ruhlmann, who may also have designed the table. Two occasional chairs are by Serge Roche.

"I always look for basic shapes and good proportions," concluded Mlle. Picasso. — BY JANE GENIESSE

TOP: *Both the living room and the bedroom open onto the garden and a stone terrace.*

ABOVE: *A baroque gold and silver conch shell is placed in a fireplace.*

RIGHT: *Mlle. Picasso used yellow-and-white pavilion fabric on the dining-room walls. The set of chairs is by E.J. Ruhlmann, the 1930s artist, who may also have designed the table.*

ULI ROSE

48

LAUREN'S LIFESTYLE
A SERENE BUT SUMPTUOUS BACKGROUND FOR A TOP TALENT AND HIS YOUNG FAMILY.

CHARLES NESBIT

W ith this, their first "real" home, the fashion designer Ralph Lauren and his wife, Ricky, felt a new stage of their lives was beginning — a time when they would do the entertaining, traveling, and collecting they had not had time for in the past. The interior designer they chose to design it was Angelo Donghia, who was intrigued both with the space — ten enormous rooms with stunning views on three sides of New York's Central Park and the skylines surrounding it — and the Laurens' embryonic notion of an

LEFT: *Ralph and Ricky Lauren in the minimal yet luxurious interior they asked Angelo Donghia to design.*

INSET: *A view of the serene, spacious living room.*

ABOVE: *The upholstery in the media room is child-resistant leather. The sofa table houses the controls for the entire home-entertainment system.*

49

interior transcending fashion in which the backgrounds and furnishings would be restful and unobtrusive.

The job entailed a complete renovation — removal of all old architectural details, re-shaping and replacing windows, doorways, and walls. The result is a celebration of light, air, and views. Yet, despite the huge windows and the lightweight materials — bamboo, fine-woven canvas — used for the furnishings in the public rooms, the place has a reassuring solidity.

This is due, in part, to the architecture, which seems to have been chiseled out of a solid plaster block, and, in part, to the fact that the furnishings are all vastly overscale. Some sofas measure forty-eight inches deep, instead of the standard thirty-six; bamboo chairs could seat two comfortably; plants have leaves the size of surfboards. The results are relaxed and refreshing, yet embracing.

While the rooms in this apartment are spare — simplicity itself — there is none of the skimpy, linear feeling that minimalist design so often exudes.

Ralph Lauren feels that the place captures the essence of the fashions he designs, even as it avoids encumbering him with reminders of his work. "It's not trying to be dandified. In fact, it's not trying to be anything except simple, beautiful, and dignified."

— BY MARILYN BETHANY

Donghia's superb sense of scale is evident throughout the apartment: Ruggedly proportioned features, such as the kitchen's work island (far left), the vanity in the master bathroom (above left), the bed with adjacent end tables, and a winding staircase (insets, left), appear to float weightlessly.

PHOTOGRAPHS BY CHARLES NESBIT

PERRY'S PLACE

MODERN WOODS AND ANTIQUES IN A BROWNSTONE

Like his clothes, American fashion designer Perry Ellis' life-style is not overdone. When he is not working, he spends time with friends, often at his brownstone on New York City's West Side. Ellis said he views the pieces of furniture in his home as friends too, and treats them with due respect. Many of them came from his parents, such as the seventeenth-century French Provincial writing table in the piano room, the Biedermeier fireplace screen, and an eighteenth-century love seat.

"My house reflects the things I grew up with," said Virginia-born and -raised Ellis. "High ceilings, wood paneling, space." Renovated under the direction of architect James Terrell, the house is a comfortable blend of contemporary and patrician American.

The downstairs bedroom has a handsome four-poster

LEFT: *The front parlor in designer Perry Ellis' Manhattan apartment is filled with eighteenth-century antiques and fine reproductions, many from Ellis' parents' home. He regards his pieces of furniture as "good friends to be cherished."*

ABOVE: *American fashion designer, Perry Ellis.*

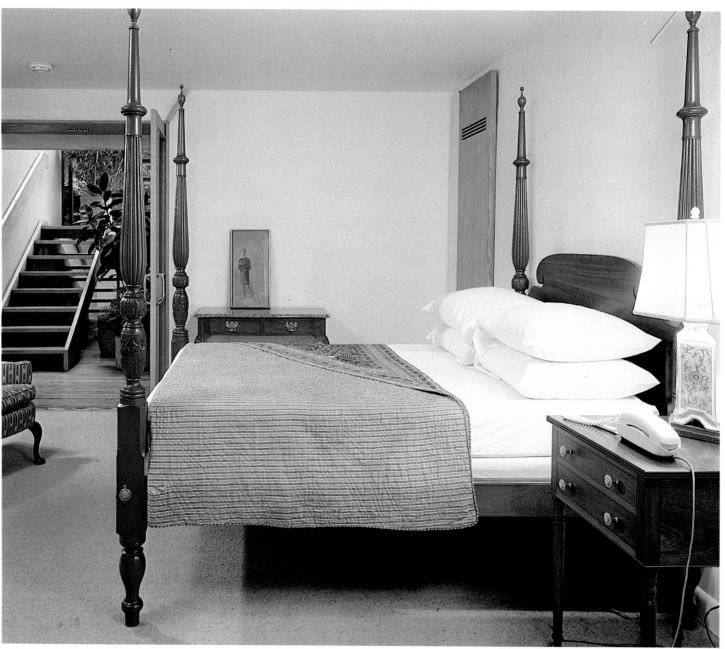

bed, covered with one of Ellis' many antique eighteenth-century quilts. But the room itself feels contemporary, with its clean lines and oak and glass doors that open onto an architecturally dramatic stairwell connecting it to the upstairs and the outside deck.

The banisters on the stairwell designed by Terrell are minimal, masculine slabs of oak that float on the walls. — BY JOHN DUKA

ABOVE: *The master bedroom's four-poster bed.*

FAR LEFT: *New and old mix in the dining room.*

LEFT: *In the bathroom, mirrored doors hide closets.*

RIGHT: *A staircase leads to a deck and the bedroom.*

MUGLER'S MODE

A SPARE SPACE WITH LOTS OF ÉLAN

Fashion designer Thierry Mugler explained the minimalism of his Paris apartment this way: "There must be room for the human body to move."

"I don't want real possession. What I need and what I wanted in this apartment was its space — and to keep it as empty as possible."

By playing with contrasts and not with objects, and by

placing everything very low — such as the symbolic frescoes by painter Keso Dekker situated at eye level — he has managed to keep a maximum of space free to be filled with light. "That is my second reason for living here," he said, "the incredible luminosity of these three rooms." His study is stripped down to the bare essentials, a threshold table and a high-tech stool facing a wall full of pinned mementos, invitations, bills, and photographs.

A key to this private world is his bedroom. There, nothing interrupts the flow of light, nothing attracts the attention of eyes in need of interior inspiration. As a matter of fact, the room's only furniture is a king-size mattress on a very low plywood stretcher. "This is all one needs in a bedroom," the designer said.
— BY JEAN-PASCAL BILLAUD

LEFT: *Fashion designer Thierry Mugler leans on the mantel in his spare, Spartan bedroom.*

BELOW: *Aside from a low-slung built-in dresser, the bedroom has only a mattress on a very low plywood stretcher. The mantel is accented with two marble balls.*

In Mugler's living room,
tables and metallic
pillow- chairs in the corners
are hardly above ground.
The eye-level, trompe l'oeil
frescoes are by his friend,
painter Keso Dekker.

PERETTI'S OBSESSION

REBUILDING A SPANISH TOWN INTO AN ARTISTS' SETTLEMENT

I t was in 1969 that the jewelry designer Elsa Peretti bought several houses for $2,000 each in San Martivell, a seventeenth-century Spanish village, ninety miles north of Barcelona, popula-tion: thirty-five. She wanted to have a base near the crafts-men who execute some of the models for her sensuous silver jewelry. Her dream was to make San Martivell into a community of artists and arti-sans, and a home for herself and her friends.

Rebuilding San Martivell occupies much of Miss Peret-ti's time in Spain. Before she bought the houses, many of the village houses were aban-doned and had fallen into disrepair. Although she never imagined she could be an ar-chitect, she worked on the de-sign and supervised most of the construction work. Her most difficult engineering problem was the swimming pool that was made from a second story of one of her houses. She gutted it and reinforced the floor and the original exterior walls and windows, making sure they were watertight, then filled the second story with water. The result is a swimming pool with an underwater window that looks out on the chicken yard. "I thought it would be so nice to swim underwater and look out at the chickens and all the village," said Elsa, "but now I find out that they all watch me."

Firewood is the main source of heat in the village, so life tends to revolve around the fireplace, espe-cially in the kitchen, where Elsa, her friends, and the vil-lagers sit around the table, eating, sipping wine, and talking.

— **BY GAYLEN MOORE**

ABOVE: *The designer Elsa Peretti.*

LEFT: *A view of the second-story swimming pool in the Spanish village that Elsa is rebuilding to create a community for artisans.*

TOP: *In her Spanish home, chairs designed by architect Gaudi.*

WITH CHILDREN

In the end, both kids and the grown-ups with whom they live want the same things out of their shared space: places to enjoy together, but also some corners to call their own. The problem is how to provide this dual togetherness and separateness with a degree of imaginative yet sensible design — often within a limited framework of square footage.

To live well in a high-rise apartment, a family with young children must exercise exceptional ingenuity. Even in the rare instances when space is not short, conflicts can arise between the dreams of adults and the reality that children impose.

"Kids are not neat," said John Saladino, a designer whose interiors are modern, elegant yet relaxed, and, when necessary, extremely practical. Not only that, but they need unprecedented storage space for all of the important belongings that grown-ups tend not to associate with gracious living.

So, he designed this apartment with a dining room that doubles as a playroom by day. "We created a time-sharing situation," he said. During the day, the plastic laminate dining table is pushed against the wall. Storage "garage" doors open, revealing a child's built-in table and a triangular nook for storing large toys. Moreover, what appears to be a section of wall swings open to expose storage shelves. In the evening when the toys are put away, the large table is pulled out or, if fewer than four are dining, a second table on a raised platform is set.

— **By Marilyn Bethany**

PHOTOGRAPHS BY NORMAN McGRATH

LEFT: *The designer created a "time-sharing situation." During the day, the large dining table is pushed aside to make space for children to play. A triangular storage "garage" opens to a children's table built into the door.*

ABOVE: *In the evening, the toys are put away and the dining table is pulled out.*

WHAT CHILDREN WANT

TODAY, DESIGNERS ARE TRYING TO PAY CLOSER HEED TO THEIR YOUNG CLIENTS' DESIRES.

One of the difficulties of designing children's rooms is that when the question "What do you want?" is posed, precious little comes out of the mouths of babes. Unlike their elders, children have not had time to form a bevy of prejudices that they can hardly wait to air. They have design preferences, to be sure, but these are often expressed more by actions than by words.

And, as it turns out, the fundamentals of good design — comfort, convenience, ambience, order — don't seem to matter much to kids at all.

For example, most children would rather sprawl on a hard floor than sit upright in comfortable chairs. As a result, the floor is the most significant surface in a child's room, more important than the furniture. Because platforms are essentially all floor, they are never more appropriate than in a child's room. But carpeting should be used judiciously. Most designers agree that the ideal floor for a child's room would be a combination of hard and carpeted surfaces: the hard areas for messy projects and toys on wheels, the carpets for lounging and gymnastic high jinks.

Whereas adults treasure arm's-reach convenience, their offspring relish any opportunity to burn off excess energy. Subtle, ambient lighting is another grown-up essential that seems to be lost on kids. "In our experience, it's virtually impossible to give children too much light," said Anthony Grammenopoulos, an architect who, with Elizabeth McClintock, designed the children's rooms shown here. In fact, children's lighting requirements have more in common with a business office than with their parents' living room.

Most unsettling to adults, however, is the fact that children place no premium whatsoever on being neat. A degree of turmoil that would madden most parents doesn't seem to threaten their children's serenity in the least.

Elizabeth McClintock rationalized children's disregard for tidiness: "When you call toys 'tools,' you understand why they need to be left out. When tools are about, a child can use them without making a conscious decision. Whim and intuition guide him from one task to another. Putting away and taking out prolongs the time between impulse and execution."

With many of these issues in mind, Elizabeth McClintock and Anthony Grammenopoulos created three possible designs for a pair of young clients, Katharyn, eight, and Isabelle, five, daughters of John and Jackie Hayman, of New York. When the sisters were presented with the cardboard models shown on this page, they opted, without hesitation, for the mounting spiral of six-foot-wide stairs, interrupted by three broad landings. The architects were surprised by their choice. "I was hoping they would choose the more minimal, off-the-floor design. It's cool and understated like the rest of the apartment," Miss McClintock said. "But, actually, I was pretty certain they'd go for the 'castles,' " referring to a pair of structures on wheels, one painted silver, the other gold, each of which contains a play or sleeping loft, a desk, shelves, and a low bed or couch. Katharyn Hayman's comment on these castlelike structures: "Too fancy, and, it's not as if it's real gold."

In fact, Katharyn and Isabelle's room is devoid of all applied decoration. The only pattern and color, aside from the blue ceiling, is that provided by their toys and art. While adults often assume that children require supergraphics or other fantasy décor, many designers' experiences run counter. "Kids are perfectly capable of creating their own fantasies without any help from us," Martin Rich, a New York architect with extensive experience designing children's rooms, maintains, pointing out that design one-liners, such as beds that resemble cars, age as gracelessly in children's rooms as anywhere else.

Yet, despite its spareness, the Hayman girls' room is a fertile landscape for play. "Most children's rooms are overprogrammed," said Elizabeth McClintock. "There are no beds here, just futons (thin, portable mattresses), which the girls can move from platform to platform themselves."

A favorite spot in the room is the space underneath the stairs. Christine Benglia Bevington, an architect who teaches at Pratt Institute, pointed out the importance of such nooks and crannies in child's play. "Old-fashioned houses inadvertently provided play opportunities — spaces under stairs and in attics that children would turn into 'tunnels,' 'caves,' and 'rivers.' Today, those so-called wasted spaces have been eliminated in the name of good, economical design. It's too bad, because children really lose."

— By Marilyn Bethany

TOO PLAIN *and a little scary to have to sleep up that high were the girls' responses to a sleeping platform with two cantilevered desks beneath.*

TOO FANCY *was Katharyn's opinion of a pair of rolling "castles," with cutouts atop. Another minus: The sisters did not want to be apart.*

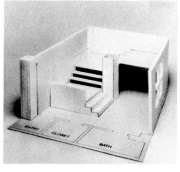

JUST RIGHT *was the verdict on a spiral of stairs. Isabelle was glad that she could sleep safely near the floor and move upstairs as she grew braver.*

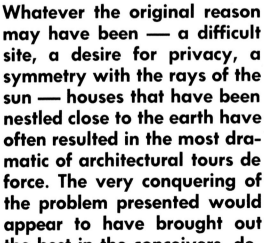

CLOSE TO THE EARTH

Whatever the original reason may have been — a difficult site, a desire for privacy, a symmetry with the rays of the sun — houses that have been nestled close to the earth have often resulted in the most dramatic of architectural tours de force. The very conquering of the problem presented would appear to have brought out the best in the conceivers, designers, and owners.

This house designed by Roland Coate, Jr., was carved out of a California hillside. Level with the hill on the approach, it opens generously to the landscape below.

PHOTOGRAPHS BY JÜRGEN HILMER

HIDDEN IN THE HILL

A LANDSCAPE SETS GUIDELINES FOR THIS UNIQUE HOUSE.

The site is a majestic hillside, rough but rolling, not far from Santa Barbara, with a splendid view of the Pacific Ocean. To have built atop the hill would have destroyed a beautiful slice of rural California; to have built at the bottom would have denied the drama of the view. So architect Roland Coate, Jr., did neither: He built the Alexander house inside the hill.

Designed for photographer and filmmaker Jesse Alexander, his wife, Nancy, and their children, this is one of the major pieces of serious residential architecture to have emerged in California in recent years. It is a concrete mass set toward the top of its

The driveway brings visitors to the top of the hill from where the house is viewed as an almost pure abstract composition of concrete towers, trees, and sky.

68

hillside site, cut into the ground in such a way that most of the rooms face downhill and are open to the land and view below. But the earth piles high above the rear of the house, rising to merge with the roof. A trio of round concrete chimneys and a "watchtower" that is largely a sculptural element are visible when the house is viewed from higher up on the hill; otherwise, the structure would almost disappear.

From below, however, the house opens generously to the landscape. Its rooms are arranged in a fanlike plan — "like stubby fingers," Coate says — so as to take advantage of as many different angles of the downhill view and to bring in as much sunlight as possible. The house is approached on a curving drive that offers glimpses of the raw concrete exterior, a set of roughly outlined, finely detailed rectangular sections which, since they have been set into the hill at various angles, appear almost to be separate structures. The road continues past the side of the house up to the roof level, where the structure recedes and the visitor is left on a flattened hilltop; only the three chimneys and the watchtower remind us that there is, indeed, a building underneath. Even more important, the four towers form a tiny sculp-

ABOVE: *The house is entered via a stair that descends from ground level to a brick-paved court. The round concrete tower, largely a sculptural element, is used as a gazebo.*

LEFT: *From another angle, the house's sculptural lines flow into a bank of lush, green grass.*

tural landscape of their own, framing the view and establishing a powerful, dignified presence.

By the time one is inside, the view has been seen from atop the house and through the house, yet the drama still comes as a surprise when it is viewed from within. The living room has interior walls of concrete and an outside wall of glass; it would be harsh but for the softness of the view, which is like a vast diorama behind glass.

The raw concrete in simple and geometric form has the dignity and power one often associates with the work of Louis Kahn. This house is rich, but like the best of Kahn's work its richness never becomes theatrical. And it never comes at the expense of a certain domestic quality. The house has a generous open kitchen, with a slatted wood floor, butcher-block counters, and a restaurant stove, elements that combine with the multi-paned glass to create a certain country-house air. Yet it never fights with the rest of the house — indeed, what is remarkable about this house is the extent to which, in spite of the formality of its plan and the nondomestic quality of its materials, it feels easy and comfortable.

So, monumental as this house is, it has a sense of deference as well, and it gives in to what is around it. The landscape sets the guidelines here, and that, more than anything else, is what makes this house right for its place, tying it to the best architectural traditions of California.
— BY PAUL GOLDBERGER

The living room has interior walls of concrete and an outside wall of glass; it would be harsh but for the softness of the view.

IN THE EARTH

THE ELEMENTS
WORK
TOGETHER IN A
CALIFORNIA
HOUSE.

T he site
was stunning but seemingly
impossible to build on: a
patch of land on the ridge of
a mountain range ripped by
hundred-mile-an-hour winds.
Moreover, the lot is adjacent
to a scenic highway, so any
plans for prospective structures had to be approved by
an architectural review board
whose mandate was to keep
the view unsullied.

For the owner, California
attorney George Norton,
salvation presented itself in
the form of Jersey Devil,
three itinerant builder-design-
ers — Steve Badanes, Jim
Adamson, and John Ringel
— with degrees (but not li-

ABOVE: *Solar collecting disks
for heating water, in a design
resembling huge spectacles,
are placed on a rise alongside
the house.*

LEFT: *A deck, complete with
hot tub, sits in a wind-free
northern yard with a planter
into which the sod roof's
excess moisture drains via the
earth-covered "snout."*

PHOTOGRAPHS BY PETER AARON © ESTO

DESPITE ITS EXTERIOR, THE INSIDE IS NOT RADICAL.

censes) in architecture, who specialize in energy-efficient houses and whose company is named for a legendary imp said to make mischief in New Jersey, the group's original headquarters.

"When I saw the site, I immediately thought of a passive-solar, earth-integrated shelter," said Badanes. However, unlike most earth shelters, which are tucked, cave-like, into the side of a hill, the house Jersey Devil proposed was to have two exposures, each of which offered an essential — sun to the south and wind protection to the north. And because it would be stone-walled and sod-roofed, it would look so natural that, from the road, it would resemble the hilltop which it would, in fact, displace. Both Norton and the review board approved.

Nearly every visual eccentricity in the Norton house has at least two good reasons for being there. The curved south wall, for example, in addition to capturing maximum sunshine, creates a relatively wind-free crook on the north side into which an outdoor deck is nestled. The sod roof not only provides highway travelers with a naturalistic view, it also insulates.

Despite the house's evident exterior eccentricities, Badanes insisted that inside it's "nothing radical, really; just a curved ranch house" with separate wings for children and adults. Though a ranch house in spirit, perhaps, its effect is something else again, thanks to a twenty-four-foot ceiling span, which is supported by exposed warehouse framing ordered from a catalog.

— BY MARILYN BETHANY

Except for the exposed ceiling supports, the interior design is conservative, suburban modern.

WITH FANTASY

Quite the opposite from those who cling close to the earth, the fantasists aspire to living in an environment that lifts them way away from it, into the land of their imagination and dreams.

In the midst of the popularity of spare modern and traditional elegance in decorating, a handful of young designers are expressing their wit in fantasy environments. These personal statements, created for themselves or for their clients, explode in humor and imagination. Living in fantasy, they say, is like taking a trip each time they open the front door.

"It's about nature and the cosmos," said designer Mario LoCicero of the cloud-studded apartment on New York's Upper West Side he created out of everyday elements — mirrors, theatrical lighting, and plants. The plants change according to the season — here, there are spring bulbs and palm trees — and the lighting effects change according to the time of day.

At night, it is most dramatic when images from a slide projector flash across a plywood cloud, mounted on the right wall. Fluorescent tubes, covered with layers of theatrical gel, look like neon. A pin spot with a magenta filter highlights the fireplace cartouche.

"I once lived in Hawaii," Mr. LoCicero said, "and I want to feel as though I still live in the tropics."
— BY NORMA SKURKA

At night, the fantasy apartment of designer Mario LoCicero is transformed by dramatic lighting effects into a tropical wonderland.

PHOTOGRAPH BY PETER AARON © ESTO

78

WITH ART.

To view a painting or sculpture or ceramic, or any fruition of a creative mind, is to experience pleasure. But to live with genuine art is to accept a special responsibility as well. Apart from the obvious obligation to take care of and protect the object, there is the responsibility to provide it with a sympathetic setting — one that shows the art off to its best advantage yet does not turn its owner's home into a museum.

Miró graphics decorate the mantelpiece in the eclectic and art-filled home of Aimé Maeght, the French art dealer and museum owner.

AN ARTFUL HOME

One fine, sunny day in 1930, an elderly gentleman wearing a pincenez and a small mustache burst into a printer's shop in Cannes, France. "Maurice Chevalier is singing at a gala and no one can print my program," said Pierre Bonnard, the artist, excitedly.

The printer produced the program with Bonnard's lithograph, and then asked what would be done with the original. "I'll probably give it away," the artist replied vaguely. The printer promptly offered to sell it for him.

Thus began the career of Aimé Maeght, the art dealer who transformed a small printing business on the Mediterranean into a multi-million-dollar international art empire.

Aimé Maeght (pronounced "mahg") is the last of his generation of art dealers who, in their dogged support of unknown and often controversial artists, have themselves become part of art history. Further, by prodding artists to create graphics that could be reproduced by the hundreds and sold at far

LEFT: *The gardens surrounding the private part of the property near the house, a tile-roofed building typical of the area.*

RIGHT: *Maeght's home abounds with art and artifacts: The staircase fittings are by Diego Giacometti; the mural is by Miró.*

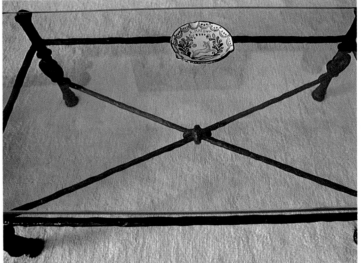

INSIDE, THE MAEGHT HOUSE IS A RIDDLE OF INTERESTING CONTRADICTIONS.

lower prices than paintings he, in effect, democratized art.

The Maeght empire comprises galleries in Paris, Zurich, Barcelona, and New York; a Paris publishing house; and the Fondation Marguerite et Aimé Maeght at Saint-Paul-de-Vence.

Maeght's stable of artists reads like a *Who's Who* of contemporary giants: Miró, Chagall, Braque, Giacometti, Steinberg, Ubac, Tapies, Tal-Coat, Lindner, to name just a few. Among the artists in the foundation's collection are Arp, Braque, Bonnard, Chagall, Sam Francis, Giacometti, Hartung, Kandinsky, Ellsworth Kelly, Léger, Matisse, Matta, Miró, Steinberg, Tapies, and Ubac, all represented by many works. Picasso is absent.

"I had the choice of Picasso or Braque; I chose Braque," Maeght said flatly. "Picasso wanted exclusivity and he was demanding. But I knew him well; we remained friends." Rather than repre-

sent Picasso, he chose everybody else.

He runs his empire as befits an autocrat, from atop a mountain at Saint-Paul-de-Vence, where he can look down the slope to the museum, and, in the distance, the sea. In a forest, he cleared trees and underbrush and planted exotic flowers, an orchard with figs, citrus trees and two varieties of avocado, and an immense collection of cactus. When dusk falls, the plants are silhouetted against the sky in living counterpoint to the thrusting sculptures of Calder and Miró. A greenhouse shelters more than a thousand orchid plants.

His home is rather ordinary looking, with the white stucco walls and red-tiled roofs that modern houses affect in this region. Inside, the house is a mass of contradictions: White slip-covered sofas sit in a living room

ABOVE: *A glass-topped table, with a stand cast by Diego Giacometti.*

LEFT: *Among the many artworks integrated into the Maeght home are an Alberto Giacometti chandelier (center) and a lintel by Georges Braque (above the alcove doorway, right.)*

decorated with a stained-glass window and lintel by Braque, a wall hanging by Miró and a chandelier by Giacometti. Walls are hung with paintings by Kandinsky, Braque, Chagall, and Bonnard, and tables are strewn with the latest gadgets — tape recorders and video and sound equipment as well as several expensive cameras.

On the stairway, the banister and carpet holders are by Diego Giacometti, the sculptor's brother who cast Alberto's works and is himself an artist of impressive talents. In recent years an elevator has been installed to the second story, and a flight of stairs leads to a small attic room and a sundeck. The upstairs guest room boasts a Léger rug and a small Kandinsky oil painting. In the master bathroom the fittings — faucets, medicine cabinet, mirror, and light fixtures — are by Giacometti, as is the ladder in the swimming pool and a bronze lizard lurking by the edge spewing water.

The billiard room has a drawing by Calder of a man playing billiards. A collection of ceramics is signed "Miró" and "Léger." A chocolate-colored Rolls-Royce gleams in the driveway.

The Saint-Paul-de-Vence site was purchased in 1950. Maeght engaged the Catalan architect, José Luis Sert, then dean of Harvard's Graduate School of Design, whose work he had been introduced to by Miró. Sert offered to do the preliminary design for free. "Together we studied the light and changed the precise direction of the museum building constantly for three years," Maeght said.

"From the beginning, a tight collaboration was established between the client and the architect," wrote Sert, explaining the gestation of the project. "It later was enlarged to include artists of the Gallerie Maeght in Paris." Every effort was made to create flexible space, respecting the dramatic natural setting and dazzling Mediterranean light.

Built of white stucco and yellow stone that had been dug on the property, the museum building is topped with white inverted arches reminiscent of a nun's coronet. Echoing the curving horns of Miró sculptures, they can be seen from many miles away.

The integration of art into the fabric of the building is itself a testimonial to the Maeghts, who commissioned a pool with Braque's mosaics, a fountain and ceramic wall sculptures by Miró, bronze furniture, lamps, and doorknobs by Diego Giacometti, a chapel (in memory of their son) decorated by Braque and Ubac.

In both architecture and landscape the Fondation Maeght is one of Europe's most inspired museums. Unlike most, it was created specifically to house art, rather than being simply a transformed palace or abandoned castle. The foundation is a joyous blending of glorious site, sensitive architecture, and incomparable natural light that celebrates art and man's creativity in a very special way. It is less a museum than a home for art.

The interplay of dazzling Mediterranean sky and cool green shade, the stark white roofs in silhouette with monumental sculptures, the open staircases and levels that permit viewing from afar without someone's head blocking the way, were all meticulously thought out.

Trails that are off limits to the public snake down the hill from the house to the foundation, merging the house, the spectacular gardens, the ateliers and guest houses, and the museum into a cohesive whole, seductive and magical and exhilarating — art amid nature.

— BY SUSAN HELLER ANDERSON

LEFT: *A portion of a Miró sculpture on the grounds.*

ABOVE: *A lily pond reflects Léger's mosaic mural.*

AN AUCTIONEER'S CHOICE LOT

NOBILITY AND LIFE HAVE RETURNED TO AN ABANDONED CHATEAU.

When Peter Wilson stepped down from his job as chairman of Sotheby Parke Bernet, the international auction house, it was in part to spend more time in his beloved Chateau de Clavery in the south of France.

"Chateau," which means "castle," is too grandiose a term to describe Clavery. It is a nice-size country house, nothing too grand. A three-story, rectangular dwelling, it has a nobility and simplicity resulting from its straightforward proportions and lack of decoration. It is tall, pink, and understated, rather like Mr. Wilson himself.

"It has real architectural quality," noted Mr. Wilson, who found the house abandoned nearly twenty years ago. The pink exterior is, in fact, made of pale red stone, each side of the house executed in a slightly different shade.

"It's an adaptation of the Italian Palladian style, reminiscent of the work of Claude Nicolas Ledoux," Mr. Wilson said, speaking of the eighteenth-century neo-classical French architect. "It was built during the revolution, and hasn't been touched since then." The interior, reflecting the same classical proportions as the exterior, has high ceilings, simple moldings, a stark but imposing staircase.

Mr. Wilson, whose conservative, Savile Row pinstripe suits are always worn with a vest and a plain white shirt, has decorated Clavery himself, not as an English country house or as a Provençal manor, but as a homey, tasteful residence filled with objects collected over a lifetime spent in the company of beautiful things.

"If you're going to decorate a house, you must have good things and bad things as well," Mr. Wilson said. "A lot of fashionable modern paintings are killers." In his sitting room at Clavery hang eighteenth-century French oil paintings. Italian and French bronzes embellish shelves and tables. In the master bedroom is a series of architectural drawings that resemble the architecture of the rooms. The effect is very simple, totally uncontrived.

As might be expected, Mr. Wilson has very definite views about furniture and decorations. "Since the turn of the century," he said, "'decorative art' has become a pejorative term; I prefer 'applied arts.' I always thought they were undervalued; they have been way behind paintings in price. They were more closely related at the turn of the century to the price of paintings. Fine furniture is, in its way, art."

While none of his furniture is of the exquisite eighteenth-century French kind that attained astronomical prices under his gavel, he has solid, handsome pieces in each room. Perhaps the most valuable thing in the house is a floor designed by Pablo Picasso, executed in white and gray stone. How it got there is part of the intriguing mystery of Clavery's history.

"The main house was built in 1790, but we're not sure of the original owner or architect," said Mr. Wilson's son Tom, who is himself an architect and who lives on the fifty-acre property in one of the five small outbuildings that are now being restored. (Another is occupied by a second son.) "The house was bought in the 1920s by an American, François Greely, who lived with a French aristocrat, Guy d'Arcy," Tom Wilson continued. "They knew the intellectual set, which is how Picasso came to do the floor in 1927. Jean Cocteau did a sculpture, which is still in the garden." The designer Emilio Terry also worked at Clavery and his decorations have been retained in the small dining room. And, in the Picasso-floored foyer, there are two plaster consoles by Terry.

"The owners also were friendly with Max Ernst and built a studio for him. He lived here before the war," Tom Wilson went on. "And Picasso dropped in one day while he was out driving. He said he had been trying to find the house for a long time

RIGHT: *Built in the south of France around 1790, the Chateau de Clavery is a straightforward stone house reminiscent of the Palladian architectural style. Gardens adjoin the house on two sides and stretch to the hillsides that flank the fifty-acre property.*

LEFT: *A rectangular reflecting pool on the grounds of the estate.*

The foyer of the house is flanked by a pair of plaster and marble consoles by the designer Emilio Terry who once worked at Clavery, but this room's dominant feature is the dramatic stone floor designed in 1927 by Pablo Picasso.

CLAVERY IS HOMEY AND FILLED WITH A LIFETIME'S COLLECTIONS.

and wanted to see his floor. He was very pleased that it was intact and said the house seemed much the same as he remembered it."

Among Clavery's attractions are its spacious gardens, which stretch to the edge of the hillside in one direction and border the house on two sides. The most dramatic feature is a pond-like pool. Originally, it was purely ornamental, but Peter Wilson has made it a functional swimming pool.

For Peter Wilson, who had been commuting to Clavery from London whenever he could get away, the recent move here was contemplated with relish and trepidation. "The house conveys the impression of a peaceful and leisurely life, which isn't true as far as I'm concerned," observed Mr. Wilson, whose unflappable demeanor as an auctioneer has set the standard for a generation and who remains a director of Sotheby's.

If anything, he has stepped up his globe-trotting activities, but Mr. Wilson still hopes to have time to putter in the gardens. In the last dozen years, he has tamed them, planting avenues bordered with cypress, pomegranate hedges, giant lotus, fragrant magnolias, and towering eucalyptus. "When I first saw it, it was incredibly overgrown. It looked so romantic," he said wistfully. "It will probably never look quite so beautiful."

— BY SUSAN HELLER
ANDERSON

LEFT: *The focal point of the dining room is a table whose pattern echoes the Picasso design on the foyer floor.*

TOP: *The sitting room is decorated with eighteenth-century French oil paintings and Italian and French bronzes.*

ABOVE: *Mr. Wilson decorated his house with handsome — but not exorbitantly priced — antique furniture.*

ON THE OPEN ROAD

Perhaps it is the sense of freedom it exudes or the power of being the driver of one's own destiny that explains why so many Americans are in love with their cars. Whatever the reasons, a great number of these automobile buffs choose to live above their tires as well, allowing them to pick up their domiciles and tool off in a camper or trailer when the urge arises.

PHOTOGRAPHS BY ROBERT LEVIN

Charles Addams — *New Yorker* magazine cartoonist, cemetery aficionado, and Bugatti racer — eyed the approaching intersection in Hampton Bays, Long Island, and kept his foot firmly on the accelerator of The Heap. "Living in The Heap is like riding on a train in the great days of the first-class Pullman cars," he was musing. "The Heap is the poor man's Lucius Beebe railroad car."

The Heap is Mr. Addams' seventeen-foot-long Dodge Sportsman Trans-Van, the Addamses' conveyance of choice for thousand-mile camping trips, journeys to automobile races, and picnic jaunts to the beach.

This is, however, no van ordinaire, and the lord of The Heap is no garden-variety R-V'er captaining a Winnebago. Mr. Addams, of

ABOVE: *The exterior of The Heap, a traveling van.*

RIGHT: *The real Addams family assembled in the van: Charles and Tee with their on-the-road companions.*

THE ADDED TOUCHES MAKE THE VEHICLE A SUITABLE ADDAMS HABITATION.

course, is the creator of the family of fiends and ghouls that first began haunting *The New Yorker* in 1937.

How, *specifically,* does The Heap differ from other vehicles? Well, perhaps it's the huge stuffed grackle, perched on the dining table, evilly eyeing the stuffed partridge poised on the wall. Or perhaps it's the spray of fragile blossoms held in the sickly green embrace of a glittering vase of Vaseline glass, a vase that once graced an antique limousine.

"I think of it as my home away from home," said Mr. Addams. He sees his Victorianization of the van as more than decoration: The touches are essential elements that make the vehicle a suitable Addams habitation. The van sports a small wine cellar, a stereo cassette player with four speakers ("Vivaldi is good driving music," said Mr. Addams), a sampler with spidery stitching that says "Home Sweet Home," and a handsome photograph of General Winfield Scott shouldering a great burden of epaulets. The van is equipped with a propane stove, a serviceable kitchen, a chemical bathroom, and fold-out beds.

Mr. Addams' co-conspirator in the travels of The Heap is his wife, known to all as "Tee." Their on-the-road companions are Alice B. Curr, Desti, Tigger, and Macy. The dogs are, on the whole, well-behaved travelers. "I think they're glad to be asked," he said.

— By Glenn Collins

Above: *The Heap sports a dark-plush interior and a small wine cellar.*

Left: *Inside The Heap, a huge stuffed grackle perches on the dining table.*

Right: *A stained-glass galley window glows with a ghostly orange light.*

ON THE WATER

Valentino's seventy-five-foot yacht.

There are two schools of thought about life on the open sea. There are those who love it damp and dangerous — positively reveling in rugged sailing that keeps them continually soggy from spray. Then there are those, like couturier Valentino, who prefer the luxury of the yacht, finding serenity in the smooth slide of their ship through, preferably, calm waters.

F or about twenty years, Valentino, the Italian designer of fashion and furnishings, favored speed boats. Then he decided to slow down and in 1980 he commissioned Cantieri San Lorenzo, the Italian boat builder, to make him a yacht that would be fast — reaching speeds of twenty-three knots — but that would satisfy his yearning for the kind of comfort that no speed boat affords. The result is the *TM,* shown on these and the following pages, a yacht that marries the graceful lines of a racing machine with interior luxury reminiscent of the British yachts of the past.

A longer, lower version of a production model, the custom-built hull of the seventy-five-foot boat is marine plywood molded into a deep V. The exterior detailing — the choice of hardware, placement of ports — exhibits the kind of facility with modern forms and materials that the

LEFT: *The artful placement of ports and selection of hardware add to the streamlined beauty of the customized exterior.*

ABOVE: *Valentino, shown at ease on the deck of his yacht, was instrumental in its design.*

world has come to expect from Italian design.

The interior, on the other hand, is full of surprises. Valentino loathes the kind of furnishings that characterize most yachts: streamlined built-ins that fairly scream their functions. Instead, he opted for real furniture, most of which he designed, and combined it with odd pieces and accessories from old yachts. Seeking a faint aura of old English vessels, he used a repetition of mahogany, leather, brass, and Vienna straw throughout. He even went so far as to design personally the interiors of the closets, which, on their exteriors, resemble shutters rather than the usual lockers. Finally, he added lithographs by Miró, Picasso, and Andy Warhol, just a few of his favorite things to take along to his favorite places — Capri, Yugoslavia, Greece, Turkey — or any Mediterranean port that suits his fancy.
— BY MARILYN PELO

Valentino's own furniture and fabric designs are used throughout the boat including the deck, which is used for al fresco meals (above left). Typical of the four staterooms is this one (center left) furnished with real furniture. The living area (left) and dining room (right) have the atmosphere of old English yachts, while the galley (above top) and bath (above) are modern but not mundane.

IN A GARDEN

A plot of earth made green with grass, bush, and tree and transformed into a brilliant bouquet with fragrant flowers is one of the joys of life. Few, however, are as splendid as this seldom-seen slice of superbly turned land near London, England.

The enormously popular Queen Mother, Her Majesty Elizabeth, has always jealously guarded her privacy, but one of the few facets of her private life that she has unhesitatingly revealed to the public has been her love of gardening. And the focus of this passion for almost five decades now has been her gardens at Royal Lodge, her private home in Windsor.

Designed and created by the Queen Mother and her late husband, King George VI, the gardens surround her house, located in an enclosure on the east side of Windsor Great Park, a royal property that includes Windsor Castle. She took over Royal Lodge in 1931 when she was Duchess of York. From that time, Royal Lodge has been her home and the favorite gathering place of the royal family.

Rarely photographed and off limits to the public, the gardens are clearly the work of an inspired amateur. The twenty-five-acre grounds — four acres of formal plantings, five acres of woodland, and the rest park land — do not conform with established

LEFT: *An imposing, pale pink rhododendron.*

RIGHT: *Her Majesty Elizabeth, Queen Mother of England, in her garden.*

CECIL BEATON/CAMERA PRESS LTD

ABOVE: *Tulips, myosotis, and lavender edge the terrace at Royal Lodge.* BELOW: *A mix of bright flowers and sculpted hedges.*

ABOVE: *A passage through a hedge leads to a wooded area beyond.* BELOW: *The tiny house given to then Princess Elizabeth has miniature gardens.*

gardening formulas, but they are examples of sensitive landscaping and thoughtful, restrained planting.

The woodland garden is an intricate series of semi-isolated spaces. Grassy paths lead to secluded glades bordered by splashy rhododendrons and fragrant azaleas. "The Queen Mother is very fond of rhododendrons and has a huge selection," according to Charles Layton, the former head gardener.

"When old plants died or there was damage, we replaced them with the same things so as not to alter the aspect of the garden," Mr. Layton said, adding that "the Queen Mother doesn't like things cut back; she likes them natural." Even in the more formal areas, the natural garden style prevails.

A shady arbor hung with honeysuckle and wisteria leads to a neatly tended, miniature formal garden. This is the setting for a fairytale house, nineteen feet high, the gift of the people of Wales to Princess Elizabeth on her sixth birthday.

A combination of tulips and myosotis is used in the mixed borders of the terrace of Royal Lodge, which are edged with lavender. Other aromatic plants, such as lemon verbena and myrtle, grow well here.

Royal Lodge looks like a flower itself, for it is painted a confectionary pink in fanciful contrast to the gray stone of the region. The house is surrounded by a wide terrace that commands sweeping views of the gardens in all directions.

Private visitors to Royal Lodge see the publicly soignée grandmother as few ever do — in her gardening get-up: brogues, baggy tweeds, and what her servants as "the Queen Mum's pea-picking hat." But even in this less-than-regal ensemble, she remains clearly the Queen Mother, for the floppy, formless hat is festooned with a diamond-and-ruby brooch.

— BY SUSAN HELLER ANDERSON

LEFT: *A grassy mall leading to Royal Lodge.*

RIGHT: *One of the blazes of scented azaleas.*

WITH COLLECTIONS

One out of three Americans does it, according to the authorities. It has been called a passion, a compulsion, or even an addiction. But by whatever name, collecting now appears to be a thriving pastime enjoyed by many. And the art of living with an accumulation of objects has led to the creation of some interesting, inventive interiors.

In a bookcase that he built as an eighth-grader, photography-gallery owner Lee Witkin now displays a collection of rare books and memorabilia.

PHOTOGRAPHS BY EVELYN HOFER

THE COMFORT OF CLUTTER

A GALLERY OWNER'S ARTFULLY ARRANGED COLLECTIONS.

Gallery owner Lee Witkin's current passion is the Tiffanyesque art glass now being produced in Santa Barbara, California, which he displays on his mantel.

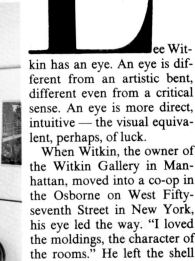

THE KEEN WITKIN EYE FOCUSES ON MANY THINGS IN ADDITION TO PHOTOGRAPHY.

Lee Witkin has an eye. An eye is different from an artistic bent, different even from a critical sense. An eye is more direct, intuitive — the visual equivalent, perhaps, of luck.

When Witkin, the owner of the Witkin Gallery in Manhattan, moved into a co-op in the Osborne on West Fifty-seventh Street in New York, his eye led the way. "I loved the moldings, the character of the rooms." He left the shell of the place much as he found it. He was unmoved by the trend among art aficionados of stripping rooms of extraneous detail and objects that might distract from their collections. "I'd languish in bare rooms," he said. "I live alone, so I look to objects for comfort and sustenance. I like the feeling of clutter around me, as long as I know and love what the clutter is composed of."

His furnishings are few and mostly of the stolid men's-club school. The dense *Gemütlichkeit* that gives the place its character "was spun through living here." Along with works by well-known photographers, Witkin's web includes family pictures, Indian artifacts, American prints and etchings, lithographs, movie posters, old toys and puzzles, signed first editions, private-press books, decorative bindings, and the art glass currently being produced by Phoenix Studios in Santa Barbara, California. "My trouble is I like everything," he said. "I'm professionally committed to photography, but I have a hard time specializing at home."

Whenever he's drawn to a new category of object, he usually buys first, then learns about it later by chatting with friends and reading a book or two. "You can't be an authority on everything," he said. "Some people turn collecting into a chore. To me it's pure joy, it's not about discipline or rigidity."

As a consequence of his free-wheeling style, some of the things Lee Witkin owns are of questionable worth, a fact that bothers him not a bit. "I'm not interested in monetary value. The glass, for example, is decorative and pleasing. I can't afford Tiffany, so I buy this. It's beautifully crafted and has all of Tiffany's iridescent intrigues, so what difference does it make that it's a revival of a former mode?"

One difference is its investment value, the eat-your-cake-and-have-it-too quality that draws so many people to collecting in the first place. "Value is subject to the vagaries of fashion," Witkin said. "When I started my gallery, Ansel Adams' prints sold for $100; now they're worth $5,000 to $10,000 each. If you love something and want to live with it, there's a good chance somebody else will, too, and the value will eventually increase."

Witkin lives only with things he loves. "I always tell people: 'Buy what you like, follow your intuition.' The collector's instinct is like sex. You can't always explain why you're attracted to someone. You just are, so that should be enough."
— BY MARILYN BETHANY

ABOVE: *Among Lee Witkin's myriad collections is one of old photographs and daguerreotypes.*

CENTER: *Another Witkin find is an elaborate console table placed in his entry hall.*

BOTTOM: *On a kitchen wall, cooking implements are mixed eclectically with photographs, posters, and other memorabilia.*

RIGHT: *On his bedroom walls, Witkin mixes media — prints, posters, and photographs.*

A PAPER CHASE

Twentieth-century avant-garde paper design and typography interest Elaine Lustig Cohen, a painter. These include manifestos for the Dada movement, printed forms used at the Bauhaus school, and letterheads, such as the one used by Frank Lloyd Wright, the architect. Once stored randomly in boxes, the papers are now categorized in portfolios and kept in a stainless-steel and glass cabinet that she designed for her dining room. "I needed flat storage that would make them easily available and would be a beautiful object to look at," she said.

— BY GEORGE O'BRIEN

ABOVE: *Elaine Lustig Cohen in her dining room beside the stainless-steel and glass cabinet she designed for her collection.*

LEFT: *Her collection includes pieces of Dada, famous letterheads, and printed forms used at the Bauhaus school for official business.*

SMALL FINDS

W hat does the museum director collect? Lisa Taylor, who heads the Cooper-Hewitt Museum, America's most comprehensive repository of decorative art, has not one but forty separate personal collections. "I like small things, things that lend themselves well to grouping," she said, "and I tend to keep them together in families." These groupings are displayed throughout the ten-room Taylor apartment on table and desk tops.

The care of small things can be demanding, but, Mrs. Taylor said, "I am fortunate to have very good storage space. It is soothing, when I have time, to dust and move my things around. And I really love to clean silver."

—BY GEORGE O'BRIEN

ABOVE: *Mrs. Taylor with a display of smoking paraphernalia.*

RIGHT: *Writing implements, including a silver desk stand from the Wiener Werkstaette, a turn-of-the-century group of Austrian designers.*

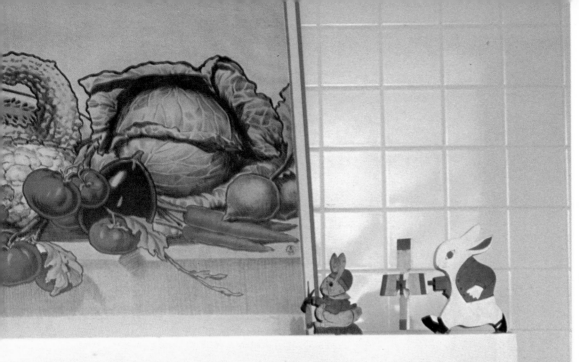

BITS AND PIECES

Cynthia O'Neal, who juggles the careers of wife, mother, and restaurant designer, has maverick interests. "If there is a theme to my collecting, I guess it is just the fact that I like it," she said.

It is in Mrs. O'Neal's large, deliberately cozy kitchen that her collections are most happily mingled. Above an open cupboard that holds her china and glass collections are two framed food advertisements from the 1920s and 30s and a group of nursery figurines. Even the staple groceries stacked on open shelves look as if they were arranged as much for eye appeal as for nutrition.

— BY GEORGE O'BRIEN

ABOVE: *The American Empire sideboard in Cynthia O'Neal's living room holds her collection of turn-of-the-century mercury glass.*

LEFT: *A large, open-shelved cupboard displays automobile teapots, a set of pressed glass, and nineteenth- and twentieth-century English and American china.*

URBAN VS. RURAL

Collectors can be influenced by where they live as to what they collect. Bill Blass, the fashion designer, for example, is an avid acquirer of many different kinds of objects. He has a formal New York City apartment and a country house that is a rambling, former eighteenth-century tavern. In the city, Mr. Blass's collections include a group of elegant nineteenth-century Japanese carved and articulated ivory crabs and crayfish. In the country, the atmosphere is informal. Here, the collections, while homey, are also of high quality. One favorite is an extensive group of nineteenth-century English and American mocha ware. In daily use, it is kept on a pine dresser in the dining room.

— BY GEORGE O'BRIEN

ABOVE: *Fashion designer Bill Blass at home in the country. The pine dresser holds his collection of nineteenth-century mocha ware.*

RIGHT: *His accumulation of carved ivory crayfish and crabs reposes on a tabletop in his New York City apartment.*

A CACHE OF POTS

Although it is only one of their more than two hundred collections, the salt-glaze stoneware of Ivan and Marilynn Karp is the most visible. The Karps, lucky enough to have heroic-size quarters — measuring 3,500 square feet — in New York's SoHo have capitalized on it by displaying their stoneware vessels on shelves that climb to the nineteen-foot ceiling of their kitchen. The Karps — he is a gallery owner; she, a professor of art — admire the painterly quality of the cobalt-blue incised decorations on their mainly early-nineteenth-century American stoneware, and they feel that the strong and simple designs are shown to their best advantage at a certain distance. The Karps' other collections, which embrace everything from cigar bands and campaign buttons to Depression glass, are neatly stowed in drawers and cabinets throughout their loft. "Our collections fall somewhere between the Smithsonian Institution and Tom Sawyer's back pocket," Marilynn Karp said. "The important thing is that we really love them all."

— BY GEORGE O'BRIEN

Marilynn and Ivan Karp in their loft kitchen, with their salt-glaze pottery collection rising above them to the nineteen-foot ceiling.

SINGLE-MINDED COLLECTIONS

Shagreen, or untanned sharkskin, was used originally in the eighteenth century as a covering for objects, but was rediscovered by French and English artisans in the Art Deco period of the 1920s and 30s. Robert Metzger, an interior designer, is intrigued with its color and its surface texture and has collected more than one hundred fifty pieces of it, including match-book covers, clocks, and an opium pipe. To display it, he designed a Lucite étagère for

the living room and has placed the rest throughout his apartment on both modern and antique pieces.

A collection of eighteenth-century bronze dogs and furniture mounts belonging to Stanley Barrows, a design professor, represents thirty years of traveling and accumulating in shops around the world. It is shown here on an inlaid Louis XV bureau in his comfortably cluttered living room.

— BY GEORGE O'BRIEN

LEFT: *Collector Robert Metzger designed a Lucite étagère for his assemblage of sharkskin covered artifacts. Among them are a group of clocks, boxes, matchbooks, and an opium pipe.*

ABOVE: *Pieces of bronze — dogs and furniture mounts — are displayed on an antique bureau in design professor Stanley Barrows' living room. Many of the pieces were brought back from trips.*

IN A LOFT
The lure of the loft is space — unfettered with walls dividing it up into conventional cubicles. In the last few years, a loft as empty acreage has emitted a siren call to the adventuresome irresistibly drawn to converting a former clothing factory, machine shop, or bottling plant into a spacious, unconventional domicile. As a result, many original interiors have evolved.

The living room of fashion designer Adri was created by interior designer Kevin Walz as an open, restful oasis, awash in serene mauve light.

Because his client was adamantly opposed to dividing the loft into rooms, he used oversized architectural elements to fill the space.

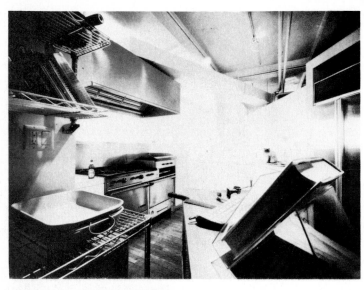

A LOFT FOR FITNESS

THE ACCOUTERMENTS REQUIRED TO BUILD A BEAUTIFUL BODY ARE INCORPORATED INTO THE DESIGN OF THIS LOFT.

When fashion designer Adri and the interior designer Kevin Walz first discussed what she required of the 4,000-square-foot space, Adri's list of must have's included a gym and a swimming pool.

"The gym was no problem," said Mr. Walz. "Adri wasn't interested in hiding the equipment, so we were able to have fun with it." Designer and client both agreed that the workout space should be adjacent to the sleeping and dressing area.

When it came to equipping the gym, Kevin Walz deferred to Adri. The New York City Buildings Department, however, looked askance at the idea of the full-size pool. Instead, he persuaded his client to settle for an oversize whirlpool bath. "The whirl-pool is large enough to float in, but small enough to qualify as a tub under the building code."

Since Adri was adamantly opposed to dividing the loft into separate rooms ("I'd at last gotten out of a conventional apartment. I really wanted open, free space"), Mr. Walz used oversized architectural elements to fill the space. "No matter how far you can see in this space," said Mr. Walz, "there is always an enormous anchor nearby."

Kevin Walz also relied on color to give the place needed warmth. Though everything appears to be white, each painted surface is actually one of five different shades. "I think if we had painted the whole place dead white, it would have looked very hard."

— **By Marilyn Bethany**

Above: *The kitchen has a pair of work islands (foreground) on wheels.*

Right: *Individual restaurant tables offer maximum flexibility, seating from eight to sixteen people.*

The gym area has a ballet barre, rings, and an exercise mat. This and the whirlpool, which dominates the center of the loft, allow its occupant to keep in shape expertly.

A MOVABLE SPACE

A FORMER FACTORY SHOWS THAT INDUSTRIAL SPACE CAN BE A FOIL FOR PERIOD FURNISHINGS.

I t's the sort of whimsical real-estate question New Yorkers love to ponder in idle moments: Given the choice, which would be preferable — an apartment in the Dakota, a town house on a cozy, tree-lined street, or an enormous sun-filled loft in a good neighborhood? Two who have actually grappled with this particular embarrassment of options are actor-producer Michael Wager and art dealer Angus Whyte. "The loft, no doubt about it," they chime. "Nothing can compare with the sense of freedom and the flexibility."

Before moving into the loft shown here, Michael Wager had lived in a five-room maisonette with a private entrance off the courtyard at the Dakota, one of Manhattan's most coveted addresses. And Angus Whyte had formerly occupied all four floors of an eighteenth-century town house on Boston's Beacon Hill — one of the most picturesque urban settings in the United States. Though each man speaks fondly of his previous home, neither gave his up with much regret.

"While I was living in a small town house, I'd find myself dreaming about a vast, open space where I could show pictures, have all my musical instruments, and still be able to move about freely," said Angus Whyte, a private art dealer and former professional harpsichordist who counts among life's essentials two grand pianos, a harpsichord, and a modern reproduction of a virginal, an Elizabethan keyboard instrument. "This place was my fantasy come true."

Michael Wager, a native New Yorker with a decidedly romantic bent, was equally vulnerable to the charms of the 55-by-110-foot space. "When I first saw this loft, I found it staggering. Here was a New York apartment where fifty people could waltz, while fifty others could engage in intimate tête-à-têtes."

In fact, the only discouraging word on the proposed move came from Michael Wager's fifteen-year-old son, Marco. "Kids are the worst snobs of all," said Wager. "I think Marco secretly enjoyed name-dropping the Dakota address." To bring his son around, Michael Wager promised Marco that, in the loft, he could have total privacy — a room of his own that no one would enter between his frequent visits. "That meant we needed four bedrooms — one for Angus, one for myself, one for Marco, and another one for guests," said Michael Wager. "It seemed that our vast space was shrinking fast."

So, architect Peter Stamberg proposed a solution especially suited to Whyte's and Wager's particular needs. "Rather than partition off a room for Marco and another one for guests, I suggested that we make these two rooms independent structures with their own windows, ceilings, and floors, and place

Architect Peter Stamberg moves one of two bedrooms-on-wheels that he designed for this loft.

PHOTOGRAPHS BY PAUL WARCHOL © ESTO

BOTH OWNERS WERE EQUALLY VULNERABLE TO THE CHARMS OF A 55-BY-110-FOOT SPACE.

them on wheels so they could be pushed about for maximum flexibility." For example, when Whyte has an art exhibition, the loft turns into the Angus Whyte Fine Arts Gallery, and the exterior walls of the rooms-on-wheels serve as flats for hanging pictures on. Then, when Wager holds an audition for a theatrical production and needs a sweep of space that approximates a stage, the rooms-on-wheels are pushed completely out of the way. Meanwhile, for normal living, the movable rooms serve as barriers between the public and private areas. And, when occupied, they are pushed near the windows, so they get lots of fresh air and light.

At first, Whyte and Wager waffled. They were afraid that rooms would be too heavy to move and confessed that they felt two modern white boxes would diminish the loft's nineteenth-century charm. But Stamberg assured them that, with the right moldings, the rooms would

blend seamlessly with the ambience they wanted to create.

As it happens, the right moldings turned out to be the same egg-and-dart dentiled type the Dakota is famous for. Stamberg used them again in Wager's bedroom — a nearly line-for-line reproduction of the one in the Dakota he had left behind. As for the shell of the loft, Stamberg opted for restoration rather than renovation — he had the capitals on the columns recast and scraped the wainscoting in the bathroom (formerly the men's and ladies' rooms of a clothing factory) of its old, crackled paint.

LEFT: *Co-owner Michael Wager's bedroom is an almost exact reproduction of his previous one in the Dakota.*

TOP: *The wainscoted bathroom was once the restroom of a clothing factory.*

RIGHT: *A rich black-and-cherrywood color scheme makes the kitchen seem old.*

THE MOVABLE WALLS SERVE SEVERAL PURPOSES; AMONG THEM, DIVIDING PUBLIC AND PRIVATE AREAS.

"The loft esthetic grew out of necessity," Peter Stamberg said. "The artists who typically lived in such spaces could only afford Sheetrock solutions and the sparsest furnishings." In this case, however, each occupant had a houseful of antique furnishings he intended to pour into the space. So Stamberg wisely shelved all preconceptions of what a 1980s New York loft ought to look like and aimed instead for the ethos of a belle epoque Parisian atelier.

Peter Stamberg's instincts were right on the mark. Whyte's and Wager's life-style is as antithetical to the roller-disco generation as their taste in furniture is. "After the recent performance of 'Fidelio,'" said Angus Whyte, "Michael and Leonard Bernstein co-hosted a party here for the Vienna State Opera. It was absolutely beautiful. Everyone waltzed till seven A.M."
— **BY MARILYN BETHANY**

Eclectic antiques give the loft the mood of a belle epoque Parisian atelier. The main living room holds two grand pianos, a harpsichord, and a virginal.

AT HOME IN A FRENCH FACTORY

THERMOS BOTTLES WERE ONCE MANUFACTURED IN THIS SPACE.

Everything in the life of Andrée Putman, the Paris-based interior designer, revolves around art, and the highly individual way her apartment has evolved is an art unto itself. The entrance hall of the

LEFT: *On the factory roof the Putmans built a greenhouse which they use as a dining room.*

BELOW: *The stairwell of the converted factory retains its iron railing. A painting by Jean Messagier provides a splash of color.*

BOTTOM: *The perfect sculptural form of a row of budding amaryllis bulbs in one window is emphasized by the stark, thin black Venetian blinds.*

MME. PUTMAN CAN BE TOTALLY SELF-SUFFICIENT IN THIS WING.

seventeenth-century apartment house where she lives with her art-editor husband, Jacques, and her two teenage children, Cyril and Olivia, is typical bourgeois French. A formal living room and dining room done in traditional style and filled with antique furniture and family mementos opens to the left of the entrance. These rooms constitute part of the original apartment occupied by the Putman family from 1960 until 1977. The new section is a former Thermos factory that occupied three floors on the opposite side of a central courtyard.

"I coveted that factory for years," said Mme. Putman.

Since both Mme. Putman and her husband use their home as a working base, they needed both individual space and a common environment. It took two years to redo the apartment and every detail was minutely worked out by Mme. Putman.

A connecting tunnel was built along the right side of the courtyard with split levels containing nestlike bedrooms, a kitchen, dining area and bath — room for the two children — all connected by amusing wooden staircases. Beyond this, a small, unobtrusive wooden door opens onto a magnificent industrial stairway lighted by an enormous skylight three floors above. M. Putman's offices are below and Mme. Putman's sanctum is above.

Mme. Putman's space is an open area, almost 40 by 40 feet square, lighted by two separate skylights and light from the center courtyard. The original factory girders and all other visible wall space were painted white. The floor is covered with fine, pale gray wool carpeting. Each piece of furniture, every object, painting, or plant has been chosen deliberately for its esthetic value.

At one end of the room are a small kitchen and bathroom, both pared to the bone for functional efficiency. Outside and above, up the iron stairway, are a greenhouse dining room and roof garden. Mme. Putman can be totally self-sufficient in this wing, and often has small, informal, candlelit dinners in her rooftop greenhouse.

Her favorite artists are represented everywhere. Sculptures, paintings, books, photographs, furniture are all parts of her collection. Since she is always on the lookout for new talent on the art and fashion scene, her apartment is an ideal showcase for her constant acquisitions.
— BY MARY RUSSELL

An area of the former loft combines a mirrored lacquer table with casually but carefully arranged objects and amaryllis plants, a Thonet bentwood chair and a triptych painting by Françoise Jordan Gassin.

WITH COUNTRY CHARM

It is a dream in the back of many a mind: a place in the country, set in rural and rustic surroundings yet not too far from town, comfortably adequate but of course not too grand, complete with all the functioning amenities but redolent with cozy charm. The English and the French have always been particularly adept at realizing this: finding, restoring, or creating country cottages and domiciles steeped in satisfying nostalgia and romance.

Vines grow through the latticework of a gazebo on the grounds of the late English decorator John Fowler's country house, Hunting Lodge.

PHOTOGRAPHS BY HORST

ENGLISH COUNTRY STYLE

COMFORTABLE LIVING IN A FOLLY BUILT BY AN EIGHTEENTH-CENTURY GENTLEMAN

Though the late John Fowler did not invent the English country-house style, he is responsible for the way we perceive that sort of decorating today. When he began his career in the 1930s, the modernist message had just begun to reach Europe's upper classes.

While the public was having its fling with modernism, Fowler, a romantic and self-taught expert on traditional English interior décor, was casting his gimlet eye over the grand interiors of the preceding two centuries, editing out the worst excesses of the Victorians and the Edwardians, and picking up threads that had been dropped more than a century before. He then codified his favorite devices — opulent draperies, modest cotton upholstery, paneling stippled or striated with color — into a style that has become one of the most enduring of our time, both in England and in the United States. In a field where ten years is a respectable life span for a style, his has endured for more than forty years, without any signs of flagging. With his partner, Lady Sibyl Colefax, he decorated many of England's stately homes and influenced the way nearly all the rest of them look. An excellent example is his own country house, Hunting Lodge, shown here.

Fowler was impatient with overly earnest décor. Though his interiors were historically correct, they never lapsed into pedantry. He preferred his opulence slightly smudged, extravagance mixed with make-do-and-mend for results at once elegant and livable. Though he appreciated simplicity, he was acquisitive himself, so he refused to believe that modern people wanted to strip their lives of extra belongings. He loved color, so he naïvely assumed anyone who didn't must be color blind.

Fowler's great achievement was to unify the hodgepodge contents of the English country home, stopping short of the "useless perfection" that he felt made rooms tiresome and stiff. He infused coldly monumental architecture with sentimental coziness. He disarmed imposing antiques gathered from throughout the empire by his clients' forebears by adding comfortable seating, fussily protected by chintz slipcovers that never quite seemed to fit. To make Fowler happy, a room had to look as though it had always been that way, exuding a quality he called "pleasing decay."

— BY MARILYN BETHANY

LEFT: *Fowler touches abound in the interior of the main house: loose slipcovers, heavily fringed upholstery, and elaborate draperies made from modest cottons.*

TOP RIGHT: *A Fowler room filled with antiques and chintz.*

CENTER: *Fowler loved color, and he believed in infusing architecture with sentimental coziness.*

RIGHT: *A front view of Hunting Lodge with parapets and sculptured, formal gardens.*

A FRENCH COUNTRY CHARMER

THE DELIGHTFUL RESTORATION OF A FAIRY-TALE HOUSE

Chantal and Bruce Thomass met as teenagers growing up in Monfort L'Amaury, near Paris; they married, and now have become a talented fashion team in the French ready-to-wear industry.

They have an atelier in Monfort, a boutique in Paris, and, adding to the aura of what seems a charmed life, they are restoring, one room at a time, a country house on a hilltop near Monfort that looks as if it were borrowed from a fairy tale.

Beyond the iron gate and stone wall stands the small, gabled house with a garden full of vegetables and herbs.

Inside the house are yards of oak floors and woodwork, old ceramic tiles, and a still unrestored, ghostly billiard room with Gothic fireplaces.

Each room is painted in pale pastels: One is a pale lemon, another a pale peach bordered in a faded mauve. Oak-framed windows are left uncurtained; here and there a hooked or Oriental rug breaks up expanses of oak-plank flooring.

There are objets d'art everywhere, each one a story that Mme. Thomass, an inveterate collector, never tires of telling. Some were expensive — a Robj porcelain lamp and fashion drawings from the 1920s. Others, thrift shop finds, cost next to nothing.

The whole house is a mélange of old and new, of taste and patience, inspiring fantasies that begin "once upon a time," and end with "happily ever after."

— BY MARY RUSSELL

LEFT: *In the living room, "where we always take tea," and throughout the house, oak woodwork and flooring have been restored to their natural* tone, *and walls are painted the palest of pastels.*

ABOVE: *The wood-gabled, porous-stone exterior of the restored 1905 cottage.*

147

TOP: *The bathroom has walls of blue and pink ceramic tile and turn-of-the-century porcelain fixtures.*

CENTER: *In the bedroom, a lacy coverlet, a Venetian mirror headboard, and a view through French doors.*

ABOVE: *An antique store-display cabinet takes on a new life in the dressing room.*

RIGHT: *In the dining area, the windows were left curtainless, and the room was designed with an artful mélange of textures, styles, and materials.*

IN SPLENDID SPACE

To begin with a shell of splendid space — be it the remains of a past glory, a newly minted gem, or any architectural jewel in between — is a sure start on living superbly well. These exterior and interior shapes and walls form a backdrop, setting the stage for the life that will be lived within. They also provide good designers with glorious backgrounds against which they can place furniture from many different periods and styles.

Architect Eleanora Peduzzi Riva transformed a sixteenth-century Italian villa into a modern home, using twentieth-century design classics. The result is a dramatic — and livable — melding of eras.

RENAISSANCE OF A VILLA

MELDING ERAS TURNS A PALACE INTO A HOME.

Four centuries of design are spanned with extraordinary élan in this villa in northern Italy, on a hill overlooking Genoa.

It was built at the end of the sixteenth century and is still resplendent with Renaissance motifs. The original, elaborate frescoes remain washed on centuries-old stone, including one in the living room by Tavarone, the Renaissance painter, of the Italian Prince Alessandro Farnese in battle. High, vaulted ceilings and trompe l'oeil arc over intricately tiled and crested mosaic floors. The crest is echoed over the doorway to the palazzo living room; on either side, cherubs repose in half-modesty. A sixteenth-century chandelier hangs from the dining room

LEFT: *Beneath the original coat of arms, echoed on the tiled floor, an arrangement of black leather seating and a gleaming, modern table anchors the enormous space of the palazzo living room.*

TOP: *On the columned loggia, with its panoramic view of Genoa, is a seating group of*

handsome modern wicker furniture.

ABOVE: *The luxurious leather sofa snakes its way through the living room beneath Tavarone's frescoes of Prince Alessandro Farnese in battle.*

ceiling. On the loggia, graceful columns frame the view of the old city.

In 1977, architect Eleanora Peduzzi Riva of Milan was asked to transform the palazzo into a workable, comfortable home. The request came from an Italian industrialist, who wanted to live there with his family.

Instead of trying to recreate some semblance of Renaissance splendor, the architect did the unexpected — she furnished the palatial interiors with twentieth-century design classics.

The merger resulted in a residence that is at once dramatic — in keeping with its majestic mandate — and eminently livable.

In the living area, a luxurious black leather sofa snakes its way through the room beneath the Tavarone fresco. An arrangement of a steel bookcase and four Breuer lounge chairs echoes the room's classic symmetry. In the dining room, chrome and glass furniture and an abstract painting rest easily under the centuries-old chandelier and vaulted ceilings. And on the columned loggia, with its panoramic view of Genoa, is a seating group of handsome modern wicker furniture.

— BY NORMA SKURKA

ABOVE: *In the dining room, chrome and glass furniture rests easily under the centuries-old chandelier and vaulted ceilings.*

RIGHT: *A linear abstract painting hangs under the painted and carved inlaid ceiling, creating a graceful contrast in artistic eras.*

MODERNIST VILLA IN OHIO

AN ARCHITECT CREATES THE FEELING OF AN OLD ESTATE.

This is no conventional villa, at least in the historical sense; it is not decorated with the stylistic paraphernalia of Renaissance palaces or Georgian mansions. It is long and white and full of glass, very much in line with the explorations of the modernist vocabulary that have preoccupied its architects, Charles Gwathmey and Robert Siegel, throughout their careers.

This Ohio house is, in fact, three houses: a main house and a pair of guest houses, separated at ground level by a large terrace and pool, but joined on the second floor by long gallery corridors that cross the terrace as bridges. Where earlier Gwathmey-Siegel houses were tight and full of interlocking spaces, this one is stretched. There is a functional reason for some of this sense of stretching out that one feels here: The family for which the house was designed has older children, and the intent was to create a separation between the generations.

From the approach to the house, with a two-car garage below one of the guest-house sections as the predominant visual element, a walkway takes the visitor under the bridgelike corridors and into the large central terrace around which the structures and the pool are grouped. The architects' intent was to have us perceive the sections of the house as making up a kind of village, little houses clustered around a central

PHOTOGRAPHS BY RICHARD PAYNE

ABOVE: *The three structures of the house and the pool are grouped around a large central terrace.*

RIGHT: *The monumental facade of the house turns toward the open land, in the tradition of great country houses.*

The two-story breakfast room, which is overlooked by a second-floor study, contains examples of the elegant cabinetwork that has become a hallmark of Gwathmey-Siegel houses.

square; as things have turned out, however, the cool, white lines of the house provide so strong an image of crisp modernism that the village imagery pales by comparison.

It is from the living hall that the real architectural point of the house becomes clear. The multi-building structure has a tendency toward rambling, despite the sharpness of its forms, and to pull it together Mr. Gwathmey and Mr. Siegel devised an immense sunscreen, a monumental structure that rises to three stories and frames the entire south facade of the house. This side, open to the land, is suddenly revealed as the house's true front — the stark entrance is merely a functional rear.

The interior spaces in the house are somewhat harder in feeling than many Gwathmey-Siegel interiors, particularly more recent ones. The owners' request to the architects was for a house that used the modernist vocabulary to create an environment that would recall very old European villas, in which floors were often of stone and spaces tended to be high and airy.

The more private rooms, such as the master bedroom suite, are somewhat softer in tone. Tucked away are some superb smaller rooms: a sitting room-balcony overlooking the main living hall and a small study overlooking the two-story breakfast room.

The house thus has a balance between spaces that are open and closed, large and small, public and private. There is a sense of great assurance to this structure, an assurance that, in the end, places this house firmly in the tradition of major country villas.

— BY PAUL GOLDBERGER

ABOVE: *A small study overlooks the two-story breakfast room.*

RIGHT: *Sunlight shafts through a window in a small bedroom.*

FAR RIGHT: *The master bathrooms are done in a rich, gray-green tile.*

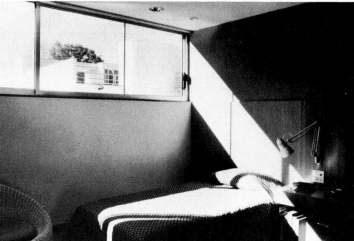

RAISING THE ROOF

BLENDING DIVERSE INFLUENCES INTO AN ORIGINAL CREATION

I n the tradition of the best architecture, the house that architect Richard Lindstrom, of the firm of Morgan & Lindstrom, built for his family on Bainbridge Island, just outside Seattle, melds influences as diverse as North American Indian and Oriental architecture without appearing to be revivalist in any way. It is a structure of stunning simplicity, yet considerable subtlety.

The idea of the Lindstrom house is not complex. Its seven rooms are set in a simple, boxy structure, which if left by itself would make a decent, if undistinguished, house. But what turned this into a serious work of architecture was Mr. Lindstrom's decision to cover the entire structure with an immense gabled roof made entirely of translucent fiberglass panels, hung from a timber frame.

The roof covers the house like a great tent, making the actual rooms appear to be a house within a house. But the roof functions on a number of

PHOTOGRAPHS BY CHRISTIAN STAUB

ABOVE: *The entrance to the house is formal, with a suggestion of American Indian structures.*
RIGHT: *The house designed by Richard Lindstrom is* basically *a wooden box beneath a wood-and-fiberglass gable, which is a practical covering as well as a symbol of shelter and home.*

162

symbolic and practical levels as well. Its immense gable calls to mind the traditional house symbolism of the peaked roof, offsetting the imagery of the stark modern box. The translucent fiberglass has a light tone that gives a diffused glow to the entire house in the sunlight, a lighting effect that plays off gently against the rich wood of the structure itself.

The house is roughly symmetrical and is based on a cross axis — visitors enter on a small private deck that leads to a central gallery that runs through the width of the house. It is an entrance of great dignity, almost noble — one is flanked by timber posts, and the view through the glass doors is of more timber posts, marching down the central gallery in even pace. The gallery is crossed by the two major rooms, a large living-dining room to the right of the gallery and a smaller family room to the left. The kitchen is tucked away in one corner, the study in another, and the bedrooms in the other two.

There are two lines of skylights running along the edges of the living-room walls and along the family-room walls, bringing natural light into these central living spaces and opening up the living spaces vertically.

The Lindstrom house manages to do what many houses of our time have attempted but few have achieved. It enhances the notion of the house as symbol of shelter without letting that symbolic role get in the way of practical concerns; it is sympathetic to regional traditions, yet it is not a slave to them. Ultimately, what distinguishes it is its lack of self-consciousness, and its absence here comes as a breath of fresh air.

— BY PAUL GOLDBERGER

LEFT: *The living room has an airy quality with decks outside and skylights open to the plastic rooftop above.*

TOP: *In the living-dining area, the diffused glow of the translucent fiberglass roof plays off gently against the rich wood of the structure.*

RIGHT: *A central gallery divides the building.*

GEOMETRIC COMFORT

A NEW STRUCTURE HAS A TURN-OF-THE-CENTURY GRACE.

The style of buildings that set off a generation of sharp, geometric beach houses with vertical cedar siding and slanted roofs is no longer something new and provocative — but it is a style that continues to reappear, and it occasionally yields buildings of significant quality.

Such a building is the house recently completed for the art patrons Doris and Alan Freedman by the architectural firm of Mayers & Schiff & Associates. It is an immense house that commands an ocean-front site

with the sort of easy assurance one tends to associate with the older summer cottages of the shingle style. The style here is based on the sharp geometrics of modernism more than on the complex textures of the shingle style, but there is a feeling nonetheless of a classic vocabulary being used.

The Freedman house is in fact two structures: a main house, set parallel to the ocean, and a smaller guest house set inland from the main house, at a slight angle to make the most of ocean views. The complex is an especially skillful piece of planning: It emerged not out of any desire to impose abstract geometrics, but out of a strong commitment to reflect the living patterns of the owners, who have three grown daughters and thus wished a

PHOTOGRAPHS BY NORMAN McGRATH

This oceanside East Hampton, New York, estate comprises a main house (left) and a two-bedroom guest cottage. There is a tunnel-like passage from the changing rooms beneath the main house to the cottage.

structure that would be flexible enough to work equally well as a house for a couple or for an entire family.

The main house consists of a master bedroom, a smaller bedroom, a huge eat-in kitchen (laid out for informal family cooking), and a two-story living room; the guest cottage has bedrooms for the other two daughters.

The layout of the structures on the site is particularly impressive: There is a progres-

sion that builds gradually from the entrance drive across potato fields to the guest house to the main house to the climax of the ocean view. There is easy movement from one part of the complex to another: Both an outside walkway and an indoor, glass-enclosed walk tie the guest house to the main house.

The exteriors are fairly simple and reflect the demands of the interior. The spaces inside this house flow with the

sort of relaxed grace one associates with the old turn-of-the-century houses of the shingle style. There is a sense of openness — every room has a view and the main living spaces open entirely into one another — but rooms are also able to function as private enclosures unto themselves. The furnishings and carpeting provide some further assistance, giving the hard edges of the structure a soft overlay. The warm gray and buff tones used in most

ABOVE: *The spaces inside the house flow with the sort of relaxed grace associated with the old turn-of-the-century houses of the shingle style.*

RIGHT: *An enclosed walk with a stairway links the guest cottage and main house.*

of the interior make the house still more relaxed, echoing rather than competing with the colors of the ocean and the dunes.

But perhaps it is as a set of individual details, rather than as any sort of grand concept, that the house is most impressive. The kitchen, for example, is intended as a focus of family life — it is large, has an expansive ocean view, and is organized around a substantial work island containing, among other things, a built-in wok.

For a long time, the modernist vocabulary tended to reject, or at least shy away from, such livability. Here, while the style is modern, the priorities seem more traditional. The Freedman house is the vocabulary of modern architecture at a certain point of maturity, not as daring as it once was, but with an air of establishment and contentment.
— BY PAUL GOLDBERGER

LEFT: *The serenely colored living room flows into dining and kitchen areas.*

ABOVE: *Although the two rooms are open, there is a sliding panel between the work section of the kitchen and the table to hide the clutter of cooking while dining.*

RIGHT: *The house incorporates such now-classic elements as large panes of glass and cedar siding.*

MIXED METAPHORS

CONVENTIONAL PARTS FUSED IN UNCONVENTIONAL WAYS

This sprawling three-bedroom house in southeastern Pennsylvania by Hugh Newell Jacobsen, the Washington architect, is at once very conventional and absolutely unconventional, at once normal and completely startling. It deals in historical allusion and visual illusion; its design is based on some conventional parts placed in an altogether unconventional whole.

The idea of the house can be described in fairly simple terms. The facade consists of seven pavilions, each shaped like a little pitched-roof house, sheathed in wooden clapboards and given multi-paned windows. Each pavilion is slightly smaller than the next, so that the seven pavilions together look as if they could slide into one another like the sections of a telescope. The wooden front and the separate pavilions are a direct reference to the farmhouses of eighteenth-century rural Pennsylvania, in which similarly styled sections of different sizes were frequently added on to accommodate growing families.

But this is no direct reproduction of an eighteenth-century Pennsylvania farmhouse. The thin sliver of the side that is visible where each successive pavilion abuts against a smaller one is covered in reflective glass, and so is the entire side of the house beside the largest pavilion at the far end. Viewed straight on from the front, the house looks like a remnant from the eighteenth century; from a few degrees to the right or left it breaks dramatically into the twenty-first.

And it is on the glass side of the house that Mr. Jacobsen's modern instincts seem to break free, unrestrained

ABOVE: *The facade of this house in southeastern Pennsylvania looks a bit like a traditional eighteenth-century farmhouse — until one looks closely. The seven, pitched-roof pavilions are stepped down in size like the sections of a telescope.*

RIGHT: *The entire south end of the house is unexpectedly sheathed with reflective glass.*

THE INTERIOR FINISHES OF THE HOUSE ARE AT ONCE SOFT AND FORMAL.

any longer by the games of historical allusion played in the front. This is one simple, unadorned wall of reflective glass, like a modern building but for its traditional shape — the profile is that of a conventional pitched-roof house. It is startling indeed to see such dramatically modern materials set within such a conventional outline. This is less a revivalist work than it is a head-on collision between two ways of making architecture; it is at once assertively historicist and aggressively modernist.

By using two such completely opposite esthetics, Mr. Jacobsen renders both of them somewhat less potent than they might have been on their own. The eighteenth-century front comes off as a playful, make-believe facade, not a real attempt at evoking the spirit of an old farmhouse; the reflective glass, for its part, is tamed, made gentle in a way that it almost never is in the commercial and institutional buildings in which we normally find it.

But if there is something of a conflict between the parts of this unusual exterior, all is resolved quite gracefully inside this house. The interior is much more characteristic of Mr. Jacobsen's earlier work: It is luxuriously modern, with a certain firm, classicizing hand giving discipline and order to everything. There is a lushness, and great comfort, in the rooms of this house; from the interior, every architectural gesture of the outside seems to make sense. The farmhouse facade effectively closes the house to the street, for example, while the glass side wall opens it to a private lawn. Similarly, the thin panes of glass in the slivers between the pavilions eliminate traditional corners in most of the rooms, providing a striking line of light instead. And the glass wall at the south end has another special function: a secondary role as a provider of solar heat.

The pavilions each reflect a function on the main floor. The largest one at the south end of the house contains the living room, and the next one is the entry and circulation space. The dining room and library occupy the third pavilion, and the kitchen and service areas are in the smaller pavilions moving toward the narrow end.

There is an air throughout of quiet, self-assured luxury; the interior is almost conservative by contrast to the exterior. It is a reminder that Hugh Jacobsen's values seem firmly rooted in the creation of comfortable living space.

— BY PAUL GOLDBERGER

LEFT: *The stairway rising through the center of the house culminates in the third-floor hallway and gives access to the guest room.*

TOP: *The starkly modern central portion of the house, containing a spiral stair, is open to the third floor and is illuminated with skylights and slivers of glass set into the roof and edges of the gable.*

CENTER: *The master bedroom has both old-style windows looking out to the front and an expanse of glass looking to the side of the house.*

RIGHT: *High in the house, set into the gable at the top of the largest of the seven pavilions, is a combination guest room and sitting-room retreat enhanced with views of the surrounding countryside.*

175

A SPANISH TRANSLATION

A PROMINENT ARCHITECT RENOVATES A FORMER CEMENT FACTORY.

All over the world, warehouses and office buildings, hotels and factories are being converted for residential use. But few projects are as striking in both scale and design as the Taller de Arquitectura Bofill, an architectural office and residence, in Sant Just D'Esvern, a suburb of Barcelona, Spain.

It is only when one is told that the buildings — which loom up like an extraordinary, austere apparition — were once a cement factory that one realizes the scope of the renovation. The cement silos themselves make up the basic architecture of the complex. The round interior spaces in the circular towers have been adapted into living and working environments.

The silos have circular stairs, and many have tall curved windows punched out of the sides. The project is the concept of Ricardo Bofill, who has been responsible over the past decade for some of the most monumental yet human projects in building and city planning in Europe.

There is both a luxuriousness and a sparseness to the spaces in the Taller that have been transformed for residential use. Mr. Bofill's apartment, situated in the center of the factory, has only two rooms — a living room/din-

ABOVE: *The architectural office and residence in a converted Spanish cement factory is striking in both design and scale.*

RIGHT: *The tall, cathedral-type arched windows are the main design element of the interior. Chairs by Antoni Gaudí surround a marble-topped table in the dining area of the architect's apartment.*

ing room; and a bedroom/ bathroom that opens onto a colonnaded terrace.

The tall, cathedral-type arched windows are the main design element of the interior. When filled in with glass, the arcades are windows; on the terrace they are a freestanding element that visually echoes the view from the inside. In the living room/dining room, they are the focal point of the dramatic space furnished with overscaled pieces of furniture.

While the leather-covered sofas are modern, the dining room chairs are by Antoni Gaudí, the Art Nouveau Spanish architect. The soft, hand-carved oak designs contrast with the other materials in the interior.

The interiors are based on a rigorous and controlled geometry. The curved shape of the windows is repeated in such details as the door frames, and the mirror over the bathroom vanity.

There is no separation be-

tween bedroom and bathroom in Mr. Bofill's bedroom and the bathtub has been placed directly under the windows that lead to the terrace.

On a floor below in the silo, a small kitchen has been installed for the use of guests and the twenty people or so who work in the architectural office. Again, there is a rigid design geometry — curved doorways and stark white set off by the graceful silhouettes of bentwood chairs.

— BY SUZANNE SLESIN

In the living room area (far left), low, leather-covered sofas are the only seating. The marble tub in the master bathroom (top left) is open to the bedroom. The half-circle of marble behind the tub (top right) and the vanity in the guest bathroom (bottom left) repeat the geometric design of the interior. In the kitchen (bottom), bentwood chairs are used around the dining table and the arched doorways echo the shape of the windows.

WIRED FOR LIVING

AN APARTMENT PAYS TRIBUTE TO THE ENGINEER'S ART.

To many interior designers, television sets, stereos, and artificial-lighting equipment are disrupting intrusions in the home and so should be banished from view.

To Robin Jacobsen, however, they are works of art, and he readily features them in his work, as is clear from the Jacobsen-designed apartment shown here. He treats the argon lighting and Advent television — as well as the view of the bridge — as decorative elements in his overall scheme. "They take the place of accessories," said Jacobsen. During the day, the view of the venerable Queensboro Bridge connecting Manhattan to Long Island is the most commanding element in the room — pre-

Designer Robin Jacobsen kept furniture to a minimum and eschewed accessories altogether so nothing would distract from an extraordinary view of the Queensboro Bridge. The cool argon lighting is balanced by warmer lights behind the banquettes.

THE FUNCTIONAL EQUIPMENT IS INTEGRATED INTO THE HANDSOME DESIGN.

cisely the effect Jacobsen was striving for.

Variety in this apartment is confined to subtle shifts in texture — from the marble of the tabletop to the wool velvet of the carpet to the quilted worsted of the banquettes. Visual confusion is prohibited; people provide the action.

And in this case, the action is considerable. The apartment is owned by Xavier, a fashionable hairdresser and a man who likes to share the comforts of home with his friends. He agrees with Jacobsen that conventional decoration is oppressive and inhibiting.

In fact, the only point on which client and designer disagreed was Xavier's conviction that he needed a dining table — a formality Jacobsen found inconsistent with his client's confessed "gypsy" style of entertaining.

However, several months after a table was installed, Xavier asked Jacobsen to take it away; he'd decided that sit-down dinners simply were not his style.

— **BY JOHN DUKA**

LEFT: *In keeping with the designer's philosophy, the lighting and media control panel is blatantly evident. Electronics expert Lee Erdman engineered the installations.*

TOP: *Jacobsen treated the Advent television as a decorative element in his overall scheme.*

ABOVE: *In the entry foyer, a diagonal wall of mirrors disguises doors into the kitchen, bedroom, and bath. Lighting designer Brian Thompson hid argon tubes behind soffits.*

IN A PROBLEM SPACE

Creating the illusion of splendid — or even suitable — space is a problem more and more city dwellers are facing as apartments are carved out of buildings built for some other purpose. Solving this riddle has led to some imaginative sleights of hand.

The studio is shaped essentially like a sow's ear — broad at one end and tapering to a blunt point at the other. Such oddly shaped rooms are becoming more and more common in New York City, a consequence of the trend toward subdividing industrial buildings into as many apartments as possible. To make these seemingly impossible spaces workable, interior designers most often resort to streamlined, custom-designed built-ins to get maximum mileage from the floor space while accommodating the awkward angles. But for Sam Watters, the decorator who owns this studio apartment, built-ins wouldn't do.

"I thought, 'If I'm going to live in a space this small, it better be amusing,'" he said. To achieve that end, Watters selected about twenty pieces from his large collection of antique furniture and positioned them strategically about the 185-square-foot space. The results are a silk purse indeed.

Watters has a special way with antiques, using them to achieve a taut clarity — the sort one normally associates with modern design. There are two steps in his decorating

LEFT: *The cocktail tables, balustrade columns topped with marble, are the only pieces of furniture that Sam Watters purchased specifically for his apartment. The sofa with fur coverlet doubles as his bed.*

THE STUDIO IS SHAPED
ESSENTIALLY LIKE A SOW'S EAR.

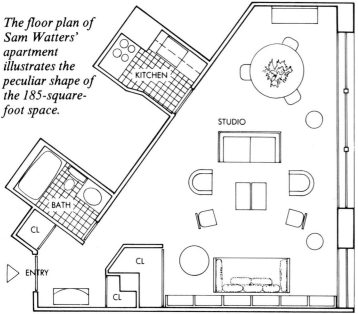

The floor plan of Sam Watters' apartment illustrates the peculiar shape of the 185-square-foot space.

approach. First, he creates a clutter-free background. In this apartment, rather than dressing up the windows with draperies, he simplifies them with horizontal blinds. He even disdains to capitalize on the imitation parquet floor; instead, he lacquers it a cool, pale gray, then adds his own touch of artifice — a bold stripe of black paint that suggests a parquet floor's ebonized border, but in a blatantly modern, graphic way.

The second step in Watters' method is the selection of the furniture. All of the pieces in this apartment are of a period: either Biedermeier or its close relative, Italian Directoire. And each piece is in the same color family: either fruitwood or matching amboina. No rugs or fussy patterns shatter the simplicity.

Sam Watters' way of using antiques is as far from the familiar eclectic approach as high Victorian is from high tech. Rather than the usual busy mix of styles and periods, Watters' method is to superimpose furnishings of a single period against a background that is clearly of another. In doing so, he brings a highly structured, modern sensibility to decorating with period furniture; he manages to fit antiques into a modern setting without compromising either element.

— BY MARILYN BETHANY

ABOVE: *A detail of the marble-topped cocktail tables with his collection of marble balls and obelisks.*

RIGHT: *To expand the sense of space and minimize awkward angles, Watters mirrored walls at each end of the oddly shaped apartment.*

IN ONE ROOM

Once considered to be the lot of students, the disadvantaged, and those just starting out, today the all-in-one room is the choice of many who like the disciplined slice of design it imposes both on the space involved and on the lives of those who reside within it.

When they designed the apartment shown here, James Maguire and his partner Melvin Dwork had to convince the owner, theatrical director Michael Kahn, that there was nothing inherently disgrace-ful about living in a studio — even though it was in a prestigious building.

"When Michael bought the apartment, it was divided into two tiny rooms, so we suggested taking down the wall," said Maguire. "He was horrified. But we proved to him that one-room living can be perfectly civilized."

As is usual when designing studio apartments, Dwork and Maguire organized the space into three basic areas — living, dining, and sleeping. Their triumph, however, is in the adaptability of each part. The bed and bay-window seat form denlike quarters for Kahn to retreat to when he is home alone, yet party guests can lounge there without any sense that they're either trespassing or cut off from the rest of the apartment. The dining area, too, is as suited to lounging as it is to dinners

LEFT: *The room is divided according to function: living (foreground), dining, and, beyond the partition, a sleeping space/library.*

RIGHT: *Full use is made of the compact cooking space.*

PHOTOGRAPHS BY JAIME ARDILES—ARCE

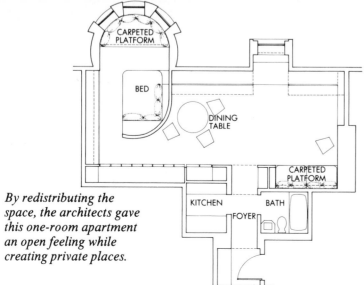

By redistributing the space, the architects gave this one-room apartment an open feeling while creating private places.

for four, thanks to chairs that look and feel as if they belong in the living room but are proportioned right for dining.

While the room features the carpeted platforms normally associated with the so-called minimalist style, the work here is not of that school. Absent is the serious leather upholstery, the high-gloss walls, the surfaces devoid of ornament. Instead, books line the walls, and paintings and bibelots are casually displayed. Though the team had read the rule book for late 70s interior de-sign that says, "Thou shalt not leave signs of life exposed to the naked eye," neither be-lieves in strong-arming clients into living in model rooms. "As soon as we leave, they're going to bring in things that will make them feel at home," said Maguire, "so we might as well allow for it in the design."
— BY MARILYN BETHANY

ABOVE: A curved, carpeted partition conceals the bed.

RIGHT: The kitchen and bath are placed off the foyer.

ON NEXT TO NOTHING

Often, economics are at the root of it, but sometimes it is just the principle of the thing. The challenge of creating an environment for living well while spending practically nothing is irresistible to many, particularly those in the design field. The results may be a bit maverick, but they are nearly always inventive and entertaining.

The majority of tenement occupants tend to do very little in terms of renovation, but David Ward, who lives in a $250-a-month apartment in the Greenwich Village area of Manhattan, is an exception. "When I first saw the place, I thought it was very small, but got fascinated with the idea of making it work," said Mr. Ward, a designer in the ma-

terials department at Skidmore, Owings & Merrill, the architectural firm.

Although he had not planned to do very much, a year ago, Mr. Ward started on his project. He decided to tear down some walls and open up the bathroom by enclosing the sink and bathtub behind a series of tiled columns that hide but do not close off the rest of the space. The toilet is in a separate partitioned alcove.

He installed a tile platform that runs the whole length of the space and applied molding to the walls. Sheets are stored in a suitcase, the kitchen is limited to a single burner for coffee, and books are kept in low piles along the wall. — **BY SUZANNE SLESIN**

PHOTOGRAPHS BY GENE MAGGIO/THE NEW YORK TIMES

LEFT: *David Ward opened up part of the bathroom in his Greenwich Village apartment.*

ABOVE: *His living room is bare bricks, low-stacked books, and minimal furnishings.*

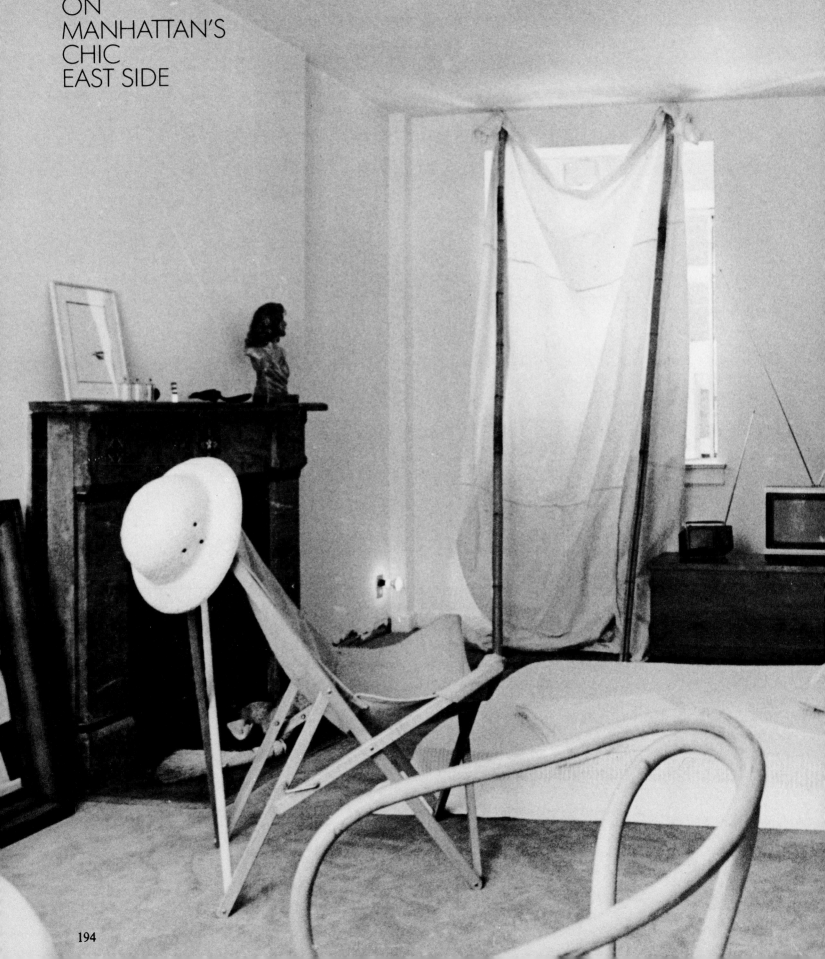

J

ulia McFarlane, who is a partner in the retail store Manhattan Ad Hoc Housewares, an emporium for practical but well-designed kitchen and dining paraphernalia, described the décor of her one-room, under $350-a-month Manhattan tenement apartment with a working fireplace as "bivouac style." She wanted wooden venetian blinds for her casement windows, but could not afford them, so she settled for canvas drop cloths knotted at the corners and hung on bamboo poles in front of the windows. The bed is a mattress on the floor, with the sheets folded nearby.

"When you live in one room, you should be neat," she said. "I'm not terribly neat, I just like to have neat heaps."

One wall is covered with Metropolitan wire shelving, and the television sits on a Shaker box. In the kitchen, Miss McFarlane removed the cabinet doors, leaving the ingredients exposed to easy reach.

— BY SUZANNE SLESIN

ABOVE: *Julia McFarlane in her one-room, "bivouac" style midtown space. Behind her are her doorless kitchen cabinets.*

LEFT: *Because she could not afford wooden blinds, she settled for an arrangement of canvas drop cloths hung on bamboo poles.*

INSIDE OUT

EXPANDING INTO THE OUTDOORS

When she moved into her minute New York City flat, Pauline Dora, one of the owners of Manhattan's Marimekko store, installed a new kitchen in a closetlike space and found room for her canopy bed in the small bedroom. She then concentrated her efforts on the back garden — by putting in plants that could survive in a nearly sunless place. "Because of the high buildings all around, I have to stick my head out the window and look up to see if the sun is shining," she said.
— BY SUZANNE SLESIN

ABOVE: *Pauline Dora, in her shady garden surrounded by taller apartment buildings.*

RIGHT: *Her canopy bed just fits into the small apartment bedroom.*

WITH TOTAL ABANDON

It takes derring-do, a devil-may-care attitude laced with some artistic skill, and a large dose of humor to create a surreal surrounding such as this. There are those who may ask, Is this an interior? Does someone live here? But indeed it is and someone does reside in it. For some, a creative chaos is the sensible solution.

Anyone walking into the Manhattan apartment of Daniel Friedman, a free-lance graphic designer, is immediately required to rethink his understanding of the natural order of things — at least in terms of interior design. Is a rock tied with pink ribbon still a rock or is it a sculpture? Are those heaped-up income-tax forms domestic detritus or a carefully considered element of the room? And what about the visitor's own coat? Slung over the arm of a chair covered with many-colored rectangles of fabric lashed together with nylon rope, it rapidly recedes from any ownership and becomes incorporated into the landscape of the extraordinary room.

In Daniel Friedman's apartment, quilted moving-van pads mingle with objets trouvés and fabric remnants. A parachute (bottom right) covers a Tiffany shade.

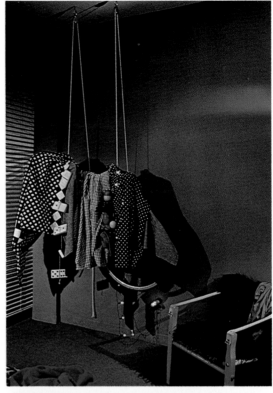

Daniel Friedman is the choreographer of this complex and always changing environment. "What am I doing? Essentially I'm reacting against what we're taught represents taste and style, and against the design of typical apartments." He gestured toward a soft sculpture topped with a still life of crushed beer cans under glass — which is also a table.

"This apartment is a visual diary," continued Mr. Friedman. "If the cat scratches a chair I leave the marks; it's part of the ongoing process of my life. I make these rooms up as I go along. I'm predisposed to looking at my surroundings in a certain way, but most of the apartment happened accidentally."

However, there is a good deal more to the space than Mr. Friedman's rather modest comments reveal. A closer inspection of a wall reveals an intricate and delicate abstract fresco of violet, purple, and brown; a piece of lined stationery taped to a door suddenly seems like a minimalist canvas. This transformation of the most mundane objects is paradoxically both lulling and disturbing.

What is most exciting about Friedman's living space is that it is, perhaps, an early example of a postmodern apartment. The old inflexible canons of "good taste" are gone, replaced by something in flux. His is an environment that does not rely on the aura of the expensive artifact. It is a dangerous but superbly considered venture into the unpredictable.

— BY PETER CARLSEN

TOP LEFT: *An impromptu hanging.*

TOP RIGHT: *Objects of all kinds hang from walls.*

BOTTOM LEFT: *An eclectic backdrop of posters sets off a creative workspace: a collection of machines, aerosol can, and scissors.*

BOTTOM RIGHT: *A desk is a still life that's rarely still.*

RIGHT: *The bed is strewn with quilts of many colors. Pillows are made from fabric scraps.*

AT THE OFFICE

For a great many people, the office is truly a home away from home. It is not only the place where they earn their daily bread, it is also a salon for entertaining, a dining room where they eat and felicitously feed friends and clients, a library where they study, and a retreat where they can reflect and perhaps even rest in peace.

THE OFFICE OF THE DEAN OF A CATHEDRAL WAS ONCE A LIBRARY.

Originally built as a bishop's residence in 1911 by the architect Ralph Adams Cram with funds donated by J. P. Morgan, Cathedral House on the grounds of the Cathedral of St. John the Divine in Manhattan was converted to offices in the 1950s by another well-known designer, Frederic Rhinelander King.

The bishop's apartment is still on the second floor, but the offices below house projects that range from an urban homesteading office to the office of the dean of the cathedral.

The latter, shown here, has belonged to the Very Reverend James Parks Morton for nine years. In that time the space, once the library of the house, has been the center of diverse projects in progress, among them, the completion of the cathedral and the attendant training programs in crafts such as stonecutting and wood and iron work, as well as solar design and visual and performing arts programs.

"It is very much a working office," Dean Morton said of the area he likens to a studio. "I wanted a space that could have meetings in it, that had a private place for me to work and exhibit a lot of things." The exhibits are primarily blueprints, charts, and designs for the cathedral as well as solar projects and personal photographs.

Grand in scale, with stone tracery over the arched, leaded-glass windows, oak beams, and a medieval-like carved fireplace, the room has a lived-in charm as a result of Dean Morton's influence. Among his additions, a collection of rocks he gathered in East Hampton and Colorado and peacock feathers from the four birds that live on the cathedral grounds.

The room has three surfaces that function as desks: a late sixteenth-century Spanish refectory table, covered with books, notes, and telephones; an elliptical table on which he keeps current books that interest him; and a turn-of-the-century English desk, which he keeps cleared for meetings and for simple, informal luncheons catered by local delicatessens.

A semi-antique Heriz rug covers the board floor in the eclectic office of the Very Reverend James Parks Morton, dean of the Cathedral of St. John the Divine. An English desk is set for an informal lunch.

ADVERTISING EXPERTISE IN A LIVING-ROOM SETTING

In 1974 when redoing her own office at the advertising firm of Wells, Rich, Greene, Mary Wells Lawrence, the board chairman, gave her designer, Arthur Smith, characteristically cogent instructions: "It should look the way Pauline de Rothschild's office would, if Pauline de Rothschild had an office." To Smith this conjured a crystal-clear image of the sort of down-played luxury and tasteful comfort for which the late Baroness de Rothschild was legendary. Mrs. Lawrence's only other request was that the focal point of the office be the comfortable seating rather than the desk. Smith complied by mixing such exquisite rarities as a William and Mary lacquer chest and some framed nineteenth-century Japanese textiles with plenty of bright upholstery. The desk — actually a Smith-designed worktable — sits unobtrusively to one side.

Mrs. Lawrence, who begins her workday at home at six thirty A.M., is in the office by nine and stays till eight P.M. She seldom leaves even for lunch, preferring instead to invite clients in. Despite all this time spent in the office, she still appreciates every detail of it.

— BY MARILYN BETHANY

A GLAMOROUS BACKGROUND FOR THE BEAUTY BUSINESS

When the fashion and makeup executive Diane Von Furstenberg began planning the offices for her fledgling cosmetics firm, she told the designers, the Switzer Group, that she wanted the interiors to look like a cross between an ocean liner and the set for an Esther Williams film. "I wanted the feeling, the mood, the colors of the big glamour movies," she said. For Miss Von Furstenberg's private office, the designers provided nail-polish-pink carpeting and a dramatic set of curving stairs that lead to a terrace. Family and friends rallied when it came time to furnish: Her father gave her the Art Nouveau desk, and her close friend and associate Olivier Gelbsmann gave her the pair of gray velvet Art Deco chairs. "So much of this business has to do with image," she said. "It is important for visitors to come away with a really strong impression of who we are."

— BY MARILYN BETHANY

ABOVE: *In the office of Mary Wells Lawrence, the focal point of the room is the comfortable seating.*

RIGHT: *The Switzer Group, designers of Diane Von Furstenberg's office, were aiming for a cross between an ocean liner and the set for an Esther Williams film.*

AN ELEGANT HOME AWAY FROM HOME

"I wanted a space that, ideally, I could do everything in," said Halston. To the busy designer, everything meant a workable studio, office, and showroom in which to hold fashion shows, as well as an elegant setting for luncheons, dinner dances, and charity benefits.

The resulting space, designed by him in collaboration with Gruzen & Partners, the architectural firm, was a huge, open room spanning the entire front floor of a Manhattan skyscraper fitted with large mirrored doors that can divide it into as many as four smaller and separate rooms. Each end of the room is a glass wall open

to its own spectacular view: On one side, the vista sweeps all of Fifth Avenue down to the Twin Towers of the World Trade Center; on the other is Central Park and Harlem. The mirrored doorwalls, depending on their angle, bounce the views along the length of the room.

To anchor the 100 foot by 26 foot area in this expanse of indoor and outdoor space, he chose red. "Living high up in New York, everything is gray," he said. "I needed something that would stabilize the space so the room wouldn't float."

The entire look of the office can be transformed in a matter of hours for its other uses with pieces stored in a separate warehouse. The props available for its transformation include more than three hundred chairs, banquettes, individual tables, and two dance floors.

A HOMEY HODGEPODGE BEHIND THE SCENES

When Beverly Sills moved her base of operations at the New York City Opera from the diva's dressing room to the director's office, a windowless enclave, she filled it with a homey hodgepodge of memorabilia and furnishings from her family homes. "I work best surrounded by things I need and love," said Miss Sills. As evidence, she has provided a desk and an overstuffed chair for her husband, the retired newspaper editor Peter Greenough. "While I'm watching a performance," she said, "Peter sits down here doing paperwork and catching the ball game on TV." For her part,

Miss Sills directs the affairs of the opera from a Victorian settee. "When the season is on, I get in at eight A.M. and leave at eleven thirty P.M. I wouldn't want to spend that much time in an officelike environment. Besides, some of the most meticulous offices belong to people who never get anything done."
— By Marilyn Bethany

LEFT: *Halston's movable mirrored walls can divide the room into smaller ones, and reflect the view from floor-to-ceiling windows at either end.*

ABOVE: *Beverly Sills decorated her office with memorabilia and furnishings from her family homes.*

ABOVE THE SHOP

For most working people, a satisfaction at the end of the day is to return to someplace removed both in spirit and location from where they have been toiling. For others, however, the closer they reside to their livelihood and its surroundings, the happier they are — a sentiment particularly understandable when the work is closely related to something for the home.

There was a time when living above the store was something less than desirable, for it implied that a separate residence was unaffordable. But times have changed. Today, more and more people yearn to live above, below, or adjacent to their businesses, a way of life that exchanges the commuter's long ride for the convenience of walking down the stairs or across the hallway. In major cities, it is not uncommon for a vacated town house or apartment to be snatched up by a neighbor whose at-home business has outgrown his present dwelling. A trend that has touched the best of neighborhoods, living above the store has become downright chic.

A case in point is Donald Bruce White, one of New York's well-known caterers, whose residence and business are both located in a five-story town house on Manhattan's fashionable East Side. The house has an eclectic past and present. Built in the late nineteenth century, the structure was remodeled in the 1920s with something like a Spanish villa in mind: tile floors, stuccolike walls, beamed ceilings. Actually the house is two buildings; the town house in front is backed by what was once a two-story studio. The structures, divided by an atrium, are connected by gallerylike passageways on two floors. The former studio building is Mr. White's personal domain. Its ground floor is a private kitchen connected by a spiral staircase to his dining room immediately above.

Except for one floor of bed-

Donald Bruce White (at the head of the table) entertains friends in his private dining room. His private dinners are often made up of dishes being considered for his firm's repertory.

rooms, the town house is used for business. The ground floor is given over to two kitchens where meals for thousands are prepared each year. (During busy seasons, Mr. White's own kitchen can be pressed into service.) The second-floor living room, used for receiving and interviewing clients, still has the trappings of the Spanish-inspired renovation: The walls are rough plaster, the ceiling has dark beams, and there is even a corner fireplace with a conical hood. A book-lined hallway connects the living room to a study in the rear, which in turn is connected by a gallery passage to Mr. White's private dining room. The top two floors of the house are used for offices and storage.

The decoration of the house is just as much a mélange. The dining room has a carved walnut mantelpiece and an oval table that could be in a provincial French house, and the paneled study with mahogany furniture and tufted sofas could be in the Cotswolds. The private kitchen agleam with copper utensils and tile floors could be in Spain.

Like many others who live above the store today, Mr. White maintains a busy work schedule that makes living where he works not only convenient but also prudent.

— BY GEORGE O'BRIEN

TOP: *The living room, used for receiving clients, retains the Spanish mood of an early renovation.*

LEFT: *The paneled, second-floor study is reminiscent of an English country house.*

ABOVE: *Professional gear is mixed with pine tables in one of two catering kitchens.*

RIGHT: *The caterer's private kitchen is agleam with copper utensils and tile floors.*

WITH 20TH-CENTURY ARTIFACTS

In a few years, they will qualify as antiques. In the meantime, they are among the pieces most hotly pursued at auctions and shops all across the country, by collectors who yearn for relics of the past at prices still within financial reach. This furniture, of various styles produced at the beginning of the century, is not only handsome in its own right, but it blends well with that of more modern design and fits right into today's interiors.

The dining room is the showplace of the Saarinen House, designed by the architect Eliel Saarinen in 1929 for the president's residence at Cranbrook Academy and still used today, with a Saarinen-designed dining table and chairs made of holly wood and inlaid with ebony.

A TIMELY RESCUE

Saarinen House, the president's home at Cranbrook Academy, the art school at Bloomfield Hills, Michigan for which the great Finnish architect Eliel Saarinen both designed the buildings and, in the 1930s, acted as president, presents a solid, plain, brick exterior to the street. But the house is, in fact, constructed around three sides of a rear courtyard that is itself open to the rolling Cranbrook campus.

There is a large foyer and an immense living room, skillfully divided into larger, formal areas and smaller, more intimate ones. The focus of the living room is an altogether remarkable fireplace of platinum-edged ceramic tile in a geometric pattern that clearly recalls Art

ABOVE: *The exterior of the Saarinen House is formal and reseved.*

RIGHT: *Eliel Saarinen designed the peacock andirons, rescued from a dump by the current residents, and the fireplace.*

Deco; sitting within the fireplace is a pair of bronze, Saarinen-designed andirons in the shape of peacocks.

When Roy Slade, the current president, and his wife, Susan, inherited the house, it had been allowed to deteriorate and the objects designed for it were scattered to such a degree that there was virtually nothing left.

With designers Jean Faulkner and Carl Magnusson, they devised a scheme to bring back as many of the original objects as could be found, and then to fill in the gaps with other pieces of modern furniture that were in some way related to Cranbrook's history. The result is deliberately eclectic.

The dining room was Saarinen's finest room, an octagonal salon with a low, round dome and windows opening to the rear courtyard. Saarinen's original furniture — a splendidly rich, round dining table made of holly wood and chairs inlaid with ebony — sits in the center.

The room has an extraordinary softness and serenity. It is lit by a brass bowl hanging from the dome which contains lights shining upward; the indirect light enhances the gentle aura of the room. It is a place where one senses the purity of modernism's original esthetic, which here, as in few other places, was allowed to develop without harshness. The low dome and the octagonal shape allude to classical forms, while the furniture relates to Art Deco; but stylistic labels, in the end, fall short — this room is an original creation.

The house is expansive and generous in its upstairs rooms, although there is only one part of the upper level to equal the architectural quality of the rooms downstairs. It is the master bathroom, and here all of the lushness and sensuousness that rest just under the surface in Saarinen's work burst forth in a dazzling array of colored tile. The bathroom is grand and comfortable. The tile has a greenish-beige hue, with black trim; Saarinen's skill was such that he brought immense warmth out of this essentially cool material. Like the dining room, the bathroom does not try to be different for the sake of being different. Rather, it uses familiar forms in such a way as to make us see them as fresh.

— BY PAUL GOLDBERGER

LEFT: *In the dining room, Eliel Saarinen's original drawing for Cranbrook Academy hangs over a Saarinen-designed sideboard.*

ABOVE: *The master bathroom is a dazzling reminder of an age when bathrooms were efficient in their materials yet sumptuous in scale.*

SIMPLY STATED

In recent years, mission oak furniture, a turn-of-the-century precursor of modern designs, has moved into the major leagues of the American auction world. In late 1980, both Christie's and Sotheby Parke Bernet for the first time included several lots of this spare, handcrafted furniture in sales at their auction houses in New York. While neither auction saw records set, prices were impressively high for this once-fashionable style, which, until lately, was living out its remaining usefulness in America's backrooms, basements, and beach houses. Eric Silver, who directed Sotheby's auction, made the point graphically in an interview following that firm's sale. "We just sold a mission reclining chair for $4,250," he said. "Ten years ago, it would have been $50."

David and Beth Cathers, owners of the mission furniture shown on these pages, remember the days of the $50 recliners. A decade ago they discovered mission oak furniture, Art Nouveau's more severe and sincere contemporary, and began putting their collecting dollars into the work of Gustav Stickley, the father of the arts and crafts movement in the United States and one of the major designers and producers of mission oak furniture.

Mission furniture, a style once favored by the likes of the architect Frank Lloyd Wright, brings a serene quality to this New Jersey living room.

PHOTOGRAPHS BY PETER CURRAN

THIS STYLE'S SIMPLE LINES ARE PRACTICAL FOR TODAY'S LIVING.

Working with a medieval-like guild of craftsmen to produce furniture by hand, Stickley employed natural white oak as the primary wood for his clean-lined, rectilinear designs inspired by those of the medieval period.

Believing the design of furniture should stress rather than obscure its method of construction, Stickley produced pieces whose connecting pinnings, mortises, and tenons were exposed as decoration. The result is design that bespeaks a reverence for simplicity and function and, at first glance, looks almost primitive in form. But the design is deceptive in its plainness, for close inspection reveals artful subtlety for the eye to savor. Said Mr. Cathers, "The more complicated the piece, the more there is to discover and learn from."
— **BY MARILYN PELO**

LEFT: *The plain lines of mission furniture belie the artful subtlety of the connecting mortises and tenons that have been left exposed, as they have been in this desk and armchair in the study of the Cathers' New Jersey home.*

TOP: *The armchair in the Cathers' study is one of the most familiar forms of the mission style and remains one of the most popular with collectors who treasure it for its comfort and practicality.*

ABOVE: *While the owners of this collection of mission furniture concede that the style mixes well with pieces of many periods, they have outfitted this dining room with furniture and accessories produced in the style's heyday.*

AN INFUSION OF DRAMA

DRAMATIC SPACE IS ENHANCED WITH MODERN ARTIFACTS.

T he apartment shown here is a startling reminder that the charms of high-rise apartments were not always so frail, and the décor is a shining and very personal example of architectural flamboyance met head on. The owners, Dianne and Irving Benson, a fashion designer and her business-partner husband whose manufacturing firm and Madison Avenue boutique are both called Dianne B., have outfitted the apartment with a mix of Art Deco, nineteenth- and twentieth-century Chinese, and early twentieth-century modernist furnishings and art. Moreover, they have used paint to exaggerate the architecture — a pastiche of real and imagined historical grandeur peculiar to New York buildings of a certain age.

When they purchased the apartment, it "looked like a haunted house," said Dianne Benson. The walls, which might once have been oyster white, had long since turned a ghastly warship gray. The baseboards, bannisters, light fixtures, and every bit of molding was covered with peeling gold-leaf paint.

The Bensons cleared away bogus suits of armor, removed crossed swords from

ABOVE: *Flanking the living-room fireplace, a pair of upholstered chairs believed to be designed by Jean Michel Francke, a master of French Art Deco furniture, are curiously compatible with a 1904 chair, a product of the Wiener Werkstaette.*

LEFT: *Before a staircase that leads to a tower room, a French Art Deco desk shares a corner of the living room with a nineteenth-century Chinese opium chair.*

PHOTOGRAPHS BY MICHAEL DUNNE

the walls, and had the north-facing living room painted a deep aubergine with moldings picked out in cream. For the small anteroom between the living and dining rooms, they commissioned murals by the artist Addison Parks. "Although Addison's gallery work is nothing like this, I asked him to do something along the lines of the Howard Chandler Christy murals in the Café des Artistes," said Mrs. Benson, referring to a New York restaurant.

Then, the Bensons set about acquiring furnishings. The only pieces they purchased in New York were a Le Corbusier dining room table and a set of Josef Hoffmann tearoom chairs. In Paris and St. Tropez, they scoured flea markets and unearthed such finds as a French Art Deco desk of macassar wood and ivory, a pair of upholstered chairs which they believe were designed by Jean Michel Frank, an acknowledged master of French Art Deco furniture, and several Lalique and venetian Liberty glass chandeliers.

In Hong Kong the Bensons found treasures from all over the Orient — a Chinese opium chair, a Tibetan altar figure, and a Chinese wedding bed which they later had enlarged to meet their Occi-dental sleeping needs.

The Bensons' best find, however, may well have been their first — the apartment itself. They were lucky to have found one that had missed being hit by the great design clean-up campaign that has been visited on this style of New York building in recent years. In the name of clarifying space, miles of moldings have been ripped from walls, turning apartments that once had some distinguishing features into so many sheet-rocked cubes. In some cases, this may have been no great loss. But in others, such as the Bensons', it would have been a terrible shame to have banished quirks which, deftly handled, contribute so much.

— BY MARILYN BETHANY

RIGHT: *Commanding a view of Manhattan rooftops, the bathtub is sunk into a red Avignon marble platform on which rest an assortment of Chinese pots and a turn-of-the-century English vase from Poole Pottery.*

BELOW: *In the master bedroom at the foot of the nineteenth-century Chinese wedding bed, which the Bensons had enlarged considerably, is a twentieth-century Chinese rug that was designed for export.*

LEFT: *In the anteroom between the living and dining rooms, the artist Addison Parks brings a dead space to life with a mural surround.*

TOP: *In the dining room, beneath an unusual pair of unsigned Korean oil paintings, irises arranged by New York florist Michael Fenner appear to be growing*

in a "swamp," a shallow, galvanized metal dish.

ABOVE: *Dianne Benson keeps her collection of ivory bracelets from Bali, Java, Sumba, Africa, and China in a Korean display case next to her bed. Above it is a lithograph by Man Ray.*

WITH COLOR

It is the cosmetic of the house and interior design world. Color can enhance or camouflage. It can create an illusion or illuminate bare bones. It can be subtle or scream for attention. In fact, color is the easiest, fastest, and most obvious factor to consider in creating a living environment.

L ondon artists Robin Levien and Tricia Stainton turned a windowless alcove off their living room into a theatrical environment for dining by raising the floor to form a stage and installing blue fluorescent lights on the dark blue walls.

The furniture in this dark blue, fluorescent-lit alcove is secondhand and minimal but the space as a whole exudes maximum drama.

SERGE KORNILOFF

BOLD PASTELS

A STARK MODERN INTERIOR IS INFUSED WITH SOFT COLOR.

To introduce color into this city studio apartment, Joe D'Urso, a designer known for his black and white interiors, looked beyond the window wall and found color. The green column reflects the verdigris of building ornaments; the blue wall echoes the sky; and the red sliding door and the brown carpet suggest sunsets and brownstones.

ABOVE: *The colors used in this city apartment echo those in the view beyond its windows.*

RIGHT: *Like the color, the Mackintosh chair in this apartment is used as art, and replaces wall paintings.*

WARM AND COOL

THE COLORING OF THE WALLS IS THE KEY TO THESE ROOMS.

In a Long Island, New York, dining room, left, designer John Saladino used color to evoke the serenity of a medieval dining hall. Mauve walls, a mottled tile floor, and an oak tabletop rubbed with aluminum paint seem stonelike in the cool north light. To soften the room and avert acoustical problems, Saladino hung an upholstered silk panel on one wall and used echo-absorbing dining chairs that he designed for Dunbar.

In contrast, designer Mario Buatta used vivid reds on the walls, accented with white moldings, in the English country-style room on the right, and played off this with a riot of color in the upholstery chintzes. "Red is a wonderful color by day," the designer said. "And by night, it enhances the complexions of the people in the room."

LEFT: *Mauve walls and an oak tabletop rubbed with aluminum paint seem stonelike in the cool northern light of this dining room.*

RIGHT: *Deep reds and whites enliven this room furnished in the English country style.*

PETER VITALE

PETER AARON © ESTO

COLOR PLAYS

ONE SHADE SET OFF AGAINST ANOTHER CREATES CONTINUITY.

In his former New York City apartment living room, designer Mario Buatta created contrast with bright yellows and blues, which themselves form a contrast with the world outside. "In the city, we live in such a drab, gray world," he said. "The place where you live should be very cheerful to come home to."

In the two living rooms at right, designer Angelo Donghia contrasted white against deep green and a mix of dark colors and rich textures against each other to create two very different moods. In one, a deep green is set off by pure white — "like a cloud against a summer lawn." "In the other," he said, "I tried to achieve the effect of a Venetianlike palace." Although very different, each room creates a sense of serenity.

LEFT: *In this room, bright yellows and blues are contrasted with each other and with the world outside this city apartment.*

TOP: *An airy feeling is created in a city apartment with the juxtaposition of white against deep green.*

RIGHT: *A collection of dark, warm colors is used here to achieve the feel of a Venetianlike palace.*

MICHAEL GRAVES

COLORING IT COMPLEX

AN ARCHITECT USES RENAISSANCE HUES TO ADD INTEREST.

Postmodernist architect Michael Graves believes that buildings should be complex and disorderly.

To achieve this inside an addition to a New Jersey house, he used color. Graves decorated the walls with pieces of fragmented moldings, and then painted them in several different colors — faded hues reminiscent of the Italian Renaissance.

On the exterior of the house, he purposely played up the difference between his elaborately painted and trellised addition and the original, simple white clapboard house, again using color.

His intention in all of this was to show that, in the face of time and chance, architecture cannot — and need not — establish perfect order.

LEFT: *On the inside of this house, the architect used several different colors on fragments of moldings to introduce complexity.*

ABOVE: *On the house's exterior, he used color again to emphasize his own trellised addition to the original white clapboard structure.*

FRANKLY FLATTERING HUES

CURVED CONTOURS AND COSMETIC COLORS ARE USED TO SOFTEN MODERN DESIGN.

Using cosmetic colors and soft, voluptuous textures, two designers known for their modern interiors create relaxed and romantic living spaces. John Saladino has created the near-impossible: the evocation of a feminine mood in a modern mode in the apartment shown above. He did it by contrasting the hard-edged architecture and unadorned windows with loose, cotton upholstery and furniture with curved lines.

Openly and honestly luxurious, the New York City apartment on the opposite page was designed by Patino-Wolf Associates as a retreat for a hard-working client. By rounding all the surfaces, from structural beams to built-in furniture, the designers created an undulating sensuousness often absent from modern interiors. They designed the cool coloring of the mauve living and entertaining areas as an effective foil for a warm and relaxing bedroom. All of the colors used here were custom-mixed, including those on the dyed leather of the Mies van der Rohe Brno chairs.

ABOVE: *By using cosmetic colors and soft textures in this room, John Saladino evokes a feminine mood in a modern setting.*

RIGHT: *Patino-Wolf Associates creates an undulating sensuousness often missing from modern design with the use of cool colorings.*

BASIC-BLACK LUXE

THE GLEAM OF BLACK LEATHER CREATES A SYBARITIC SETTING.

Carpeted walls and floors, leather seating, and travertine surfaces, all done in luxurious and elegant black, bring to this living area a Sybaritic look that belies the inherent practicality of the materials. Designed by Patino-Wolf Associates for a young Long Island, New York, couple, the space is flexibly organized to serve a range of activities.

Black has been used in this sculptural room as the ultimate in voluptuous color to enhance the rich materials and smoothed textures.

THE PRODUCERS, AUTHORS, & PHOTOGRAPHERS

To some people, home design, decoration, architecture, and style are not subjective sorts of things; they are the stuff of their workaday lives. The critics, reporters, editors, and photographers whose brief biographies appear here and on the following pages have turned their professional eyes — some occasionally, most on a regular basis — to chronicling the world of the well-lived life. Their observations are what make up this book.

CARRIE DONOVAN

The senior editor for the life-style sections of *The New York Times Magazine* and the editor of this book has one decorating dictum: "If you believe in something, you should really *do* it," which perhaps explains why everything, including the tables, in her Manhattan living-dining-working area is slipcovered in one orange cotton print. She described this space as "sort of a sun porch," since all of the surfaces not covered with collections of photographs, personal mementos, and books and magazines are laden with plants. Like most people who love clutter, she dreads the thought of ever having to move, or, for that matter, to repaint.

MICHAEL VALENTI

Mr. Valenti is a designer on *The New York Times Magazine* and the art director of this book.

He lives in a small loft in Manhattan's Greenwich Village with his wife, Sophie, and their two children, Alexander and Gabrielle.

He not only subscribes to the practice of white walls to compensate for the lack of windows in the city, he has also, for the past thirteen years and three apartments, had a white floor. The loft is otherwise sparsely yet comfortably furnished.

ALISON MacFARLANE

Ms. MacFarlane divides her time between her Brooklyn garden apartment, an ever-changing environment of furniture, flowers, and artifacts, where the emphasis is on color and comfort, and her home-away-from-home, a pied-à-terre on the eighth floor of *The New York Times* building fashioned out of a beige, built-in bookcase and a steel locker.

She is copy editor for *The New York Times* special Part Twos as well as managing editor for this book, and a freelance reporter, writer, and copy editor.

MELANIE FLEISCHMANN

Her small New York City apartment tries valiantly to accomodate a growing collection of "treasures" and other paraphernalia, some of which is decorative, and some of which is distinctly not so decorative. But the real attraction is the large terrace garden, which grows enthusiastically, doing its utmost to keep her from moving to the country where she could have a proper garden. Miss Fleischmann is a reporter for the Home Design and Home Entertaining special Part Twos of *The New York Times Magazine*. She also contributes to the paper's Home Section and was a key cog in collecting material for this book.

MARILYN BETHANY

Marilyn Bethany, design editor of *The New York Times Magazine,* and her husband, Edward Tivnan, a writer and television producer, divide their time between a half-decorated apartment in Greenwich Village (shown here) and a half-restored, 150-year-old whaler's house in Sag Harbor, Long Island. "Plaster dust is in my blood," she said. "My parents were compulsive redoers, too. However, I intend to instill in our daughter, Maisie, the sense to leave well enough alone."

PAUL GOLDBERGER

The architecture critic of *The New York Times,* he once lived in the Dakota, the landmark New York City residence. He recently moved to a large apartment building built in the 1930s and has found the layout of the apartment surprisingly comfortable. He is presently discovering, he said, "the joys of conventional living space."

He is the author of *The City Observed — New York: An Architectural Guide to Manhattan,* published in 1979, and is presently at work on a visual history of the skyscraper to be published in 1981.

SUZANNE SLESIN

Suzanne Slesin, the assistant editor of The Home Section of *The New York Times,* and the co-author of *High-Tech, the Industrial Style and Source Book for the Home,* has been a design reporter and home furnishings editor for the last twelve years. A born New Yorker, she lives with her husband, Michael Steinberg, a writer, in a Manhattan apartment furnished with early 1950s Pierre Jeanneret chairs and late 1970s metal library shelving. A recent acquisition is the circular wrought-iron banquette that used to grace the downstairs lobby of the Trans-Lux 85th Street movie theatre. The beagle's name is Gladys.

GEORGE O'BRIEN

A San Franciscan by birth, Mr. O'Brien has worked as a reporter and writer on design matters for various publications, including a stint in the 1960s as Home News editor for *The New York Times* where he produced the first *New York Times Book of Design and Decoration.* A former vice president and design director of Tiffany & Co., he is now a design consultant and writes frequently on the subject of good interiors.

He divides his time between a Manhattan apartment and a house in New Jersey, both of which have spare, immaculate, handsome interiors. He entertains handsomely in both.

NANCY BUIRSKI

SUSAN HELLER ANDERSON

Susan Heller Anderson was born in Boston, Mass. and educated in Los Angeles. For the past decade, she has been settled in Europe, living in Paris and commuting regularly to London, filing a steady stream of stories on the good life to *The New York Times.*

In Paris, she lives in a charming mews house filled with books, an impressive collection of phonograph records and old Vuitton steamer trunks, one Cuisinart, and practically no furniture.

She has a son at school in Boston.

PETER CARLSEN

Living well in any great city, Mr. Carlsen believes, is largely a question of editing. "I tend to agree with Chanel, who I think is probably one of the great, if enigmatic, women of the century, that 'one should throw out something every day.' I may not quite manage a daily ritual, but I do aim for, say, a monthly cleansing process."

"As for luxury," he said, "I'll take the following: Masses of natural light. Silence. And a view. Some people might add spaciousness but not I. I'm happy in a compact, concentrated space, as long as it's intelligently ordered and harmonious."

Mr. Carlsen is a writer specializing in interior design and men's fashion.

GENE MAGGIO/THE NEW YORK TIMES

GLENN COLLINS

Glenn Collins, a columnist for the Style section of *The New York Times,* inhabits a six-room apartment in Manhattan with his wife, Sarah, and their two children. "The decor," he said, "might best be described as low-tech." He is not a van-er like Charles Addams, but rather an avid marathoner whose dream, he said, "is to circuit the basement of the Cooper-Hewitt Museum in a running time fast enough to avoid becoming part of the permanent collection."

ARTHUR ELGORT

JOHN DUKA

Mr. Duka is a columnist and reporter for the Style section of *The New York Times.*

He graduated from the Medill School of Journalism at Northwestern and did graduate work at the Accademia delle Belle Arte in Florence, and his writings have been published in various publications.

His rule for living well is to sleep with his Sony at the foot of his bed, his stereo at his head, and to keep all the controls by his pillow.

JANE
GENIESSE

Jane Geniesse worked as a reporter on two now defunct newspapers, the *World-Telegram & Sun* and the *Boston Herald*, but she disclaims emphatically any responsibility for their demise.

After marriage to Robert J. Geniesse and the arrival of two babies, she withdrew to her apartment and took up a career as a freelance writer. She wishes she did not have to spend most of the time in the apartment in New York City overlooking Central Park so that she could spend more time in her country glass house overlooking a pond with two swans.

She is the author of a novel, *The Riches of Life*.

MARILYN
PELO

Marilyn Pelo lives with her husband in a 1903 brownstone in Hell's Kitchen, a ghetto-on-the-rise in Manhattan. The apartment is a "railroad" — six small rooms lined up one behind the other — with no separate bedroom, no closets, and no doors between rooms — a challenge that she enjoys.

She believes it's a cinch to give the impression of living well in an inner-city neighborhood. "When guests enter my country-style kitchen after walking through our rundown neighborhood and the old building's dark halls, they think they are in heaven." She is deputy to the life-style editor of *The New York Times Magazine* and also writes on design.

MARY
RUSSELL

A photo-journalist who works in a constant cycle between Paris and Milan, Milan and New York, and points in between, Miss Russell commutes between a walk-up flat on Rue de Furstenberg in Paris, a walk-up apartment on Manhattan's East Side, and an 1845 colonial wood-frame house on the village green of a Long Island town.

"I love to bounce back and forth across the ocean," she said, "to contrast one culture against the other."

NORMA
SKURKA

She is the former executive editor of *House Beautiful*, and once the Home editor of *The New York Times Magazine*.

She has a Manhattan apartment and a 100-year-old farmhouse in upstate New York, which she is restoring. She has worked with so much color and pattern that her own digs tend to be white, and even her two dogs are white. She knew her apartment was just right when a decorator friend offered to give her his clients' cast-off furniture.

She is the author of *Design for a Limited Planet, Underground Interiors* and *The New York Times Book of Interior Design and Decoration*.

PETER AARON

Mr. Aaron studied organic chemistry at St. Edmund Hall, Oxford University, and received a BA in physics from Bard College. In 1971, he received an MFA from the New York University Institute of Film and Television. From 1972 to 1975, he served as an apprentice to Ezra Stoller, the dean of architectural photographers.

He has worked on numerous film projects and his photographs have appeared in a number of publications.

JAIME ARDILES-ARCE

Born in La Paz, Bolivia, he was originally an architect by profession and worked in the offices of Marcel Breuer. He received his architectural degree from Columbia University. An avid traveler, his work in fashion and travel photography as well as architecture and interior design has taken him to three continents.

He described his approach to photographing interiors as using "embellished existing light." He believes that a photographer's obligation is not only to show the physical aspects of a building or interior, but to communicate the feeling — "the sensuality" — of a space.

CARLA DE BENEDETTI

Carla de Benedetti studied architecture but then, following a course in photography, began to specialize in photographing architecture and interiors. In the past twenty years, her work has appeared in most major European magazines, as well as those in this country.

Based in Milan, she travels extensively and photographs subjects that "concern the organization of space — including agricultural and scientific projects."

RALPH BOGERTMAN

He first got his hands on a camera while working for Army Intelligence in Vietnam. After that, Mr. Bogertman said, "I went straight to Hong Kong and bought myself a whole bunch of equipment."

Mr. Bogertman's New York City studio is filled with furniture that he made himself out of terra cotta pipes, roof tiles, sewer tiles, and formica slabs. "A photographer gets to be a kind of problem solver," he said, "and I've wound up building a lot of sets. So now I can build almost anything." He is also a carpenter and a welder and says that the next thing he is going to tackle is house building.

ELIZABETH ZESCHIN

CHRIS CALLIS

While in a fraternity at the University of California at Davis, where he received a B.S. in food science, Mr. Callis started taking party pictures and fell in love with photography. After a session in the Famous Photographer's correspondence course and three years of Army photography at Fort Sill, Oklahoma and in Vietnam, he attended the Art Center College of Design.

He opened a studio in New York in 1974, and works now as an editorial, album-cover and room-interior photographer. "I'm very nosey," he said. "I love to hear people's life stories and snoop around people's homes."

RICHARD CHAMPION

Born in Texas, Richard Champion was educated at Northwestern and Louisiana State University in landscape design and ornamental horticulture. As a licensed teacher in New York State, he taught school there while photographing landscapes. This led to architectural photography and interiors, both closely related to landscaping.

But, he said, "I've grown to feel that landscapes mostly belong outdoors and that rooms are probably more livable with less plant life unless you are truly interested in growing a garden — otherwise save the space for living and keep only a bunch of fresh blooms nearby for your touch of nature."

© LISA CUSHMAN

PETER CURRAN

Brought up in upstate New York, Mr. Curran studied photography at the Rhode Island School of Design. His teachers there were Aaron Siskind and Harry Callahan. Since graduating in 1975, he has been a regular contributor to *The New York Times Magazine,* and his work has also appeared in various other publications.

His assignments have taken him to Europe and the Far East.

When not photographing, Mr. Curran can be found aboard his sloop *Madison Avenue.* He and his wife live in New York City with no children, no cats, no dogs, and absolutely no cows.

MICHAEL DUNNE

Although he started photographing interiors in 1974, Mr. Dunne is best known in Europe for his fashion photography.

He divides his life between England, Europe, the United States, Africa, the Middle East, and Australia. In England, Mr. Dunne lives with his wife, Mary, third daughter of Baron Lord Rennell of Rodd, a painter and etcher under her maiden name, Mary Rodd, and their five children. They have a London house and a farm in the West Country that is only slightly modernized; otherwise it has been untouched since it had new additions in 1652. He takes to the farming life very happily.

248

HENRY L. FECHTMAN

JÜRGEN HILMER

Mr. Hilmer said that his photographs of architecture depend not only on careful planning but on patience and on some added element — perhaps luck — to make an image exceptional. His goal is to capture the form and personality of a piece of architecture in the two dimensions of a photograph and to add, with professional skills, drama and impact.

The work of this European-born photographer has been exhibited at the Museum of Modern Art in San Francisco and has won many awards. He has his own photography business and is photographic director of *The Santa Barbara Magazine* in California.

HIRO

Born Yasuhiro Wakabayashi in Shanghai, Hiro lived in Peking and Tokyo. In 1954, he came to New York and worked for the renowned art director Alexey Brodovitch and the photographer Richard Avedon. Now one of the best known American photographers, particularly of still-life and portraits, he rarely photographs interiors, but he brings to them the same clear, logical eye he brings to his other subjects.

Hiro is currently designing a penthouse home in a landmark Manhattan building, and divides his time between this and a retreat on a lake in the Canadian wilderness. He and his wife have two sons.

WILL FALLER

EVELYN HOFER

Ms. Hofer has been called one of the living masters of her medium by Hilton Kramer, art critic of *The New York Times*. Born in Germany, she spent her childhood in Spain and Switzerland. In Switzerland during the war, there was not time for an art education, so she turned to photography. After the war, she moved to Mexico, and in 1947, came to New York City. She continues to live in Manhattan while traveling widely.

Her books include *The Stones of Florence, London Perceived, The Presence of Spain, New York Proclaimed, The Evidence of Washington,* and *Dublin: A Portrait.*

IAN GRAHAM

HORST

One of the most renowned photographers of fashionable luminaries, as well as of interiors, Horst P. Horst, known professionally as simply Horst, studied art in Hamburg and architecture with Le Corbusier in Paris before he became a photographer.

Although he travels constantly, his base is a charming house on Long Island's North Shore with an enviable garden. He is an avid gardener.

His books include *Photographs of a Decade, Patterns from Nature, Orientals,* and *Salute to the Thirties.*

He is currently writing an autobiography.

SERGE KORNILOFF

Born in Paris of Russian parents, he has always been interested in photography and has been practicing it since he was nineteen. He first did fashion photography and does not remember how or when he got into recording interiors. His own apartment, he said, "is not at all like those I photograph."

Because he travels

constantly, his three-room Paris flat is mainly a place to drop one bag and pick up another. It is very functional with no decoration. In addition, he is continually moving. "I never stay more than six months to a year in one apartment," he said. "And even these spaces are always changing."

ROBERT J. LEVIN

Mr. Levin was born in Brooklyn and received a Bachelor of Industrial Design from Pratt Institute in 1971. He taught photography and aesthetics at Pratt, and basic photography at the Germain School of Photography. From 1979 to 1980, he was a *Times* staff photographer, photographing architecture, interiors, and portraits

primarily for the Home and Living sections. He is currently working as a freelance photographer for *The Times.*

He has had exhibitions in New York City, Santa Barbara, California, Baltimore, and Brooklyn, and his work is included in the Museum of Modern Art and private collections.

GENE MAGGIO

Gene Maggio was born and raised in New Jersey, where his father ran a small, family-oriented photo studio. At an early age, he developed his interest in photography and learned the basics. Drafted into the United States Army in 1951, he worked as the Sixth Infantry regimental photographer in Berlin, Germany.

Afterwards, he attended the Rochester Institute of Technology, receiving a degree in photographic technology. He joined *The New York Times* studio in 1955. He is currently working for *The Times,* covering a variety of assignments for all departments of the paper.

NORMAN McGRATH

Exposed to architecture by his architect father, Mr. McGrath studied civil engineering at Dublin's Trinity College, which has no school of architecture. He practiced in consulting engineering firms before becoming involved in photography and turned to the documentation of architecture in the sixties.

"In spite of people's mobility in the later half of the twentieth century," he said, "the world's most important man-made structures are probably best known by photographic images of them. The photographic interpretation of the building or space thus becomes the most enduring image."

DERRY
MOORE

In private life, he is Lord Moore and a relative of the English royal family.

He lives with his wife on a street in Notting Hill Gate, in a duplex built in the 1840s that is filled with funny old Indian prints, of which he is especially fond, and Bloomsbury prints.

A well-known photographer whose photographs have appeared in several publications, he has published a book on houses in Los Angeles called *The Dream Come True,* with a text by Brendan Gill, and his book on royal gardens is being published in 1981. He is currently working on a book on houses in Washington which is to be published next year.

CHARLES
NESBIT

Born in Wytheville, Virginia, he lived in Richmond until 1966. He received his BA in English from Yale University in 1970 and an MFA in photography from Yale University School of Art in 1974.

He has worked as a freelance photographer's assistant to Arthur Elgort, John Hill, Barry Lategan, Theo, John Vidol, Albert Watson, and Bruce Weber.

He lives in a small, cluttered studio with oriental rugs and no furniture. A category-free racer, he trains five to six days a week and, when possible, sails on weekends.

RICHARD
PAYNE

After studying photography in Germany, Mr. Payne received a Bachelor of Architecture degree from Texas Tech University. He then worked as a designer for firms in Texas until 1968, when he began photographing architecture.

He has photographed projects for architects throughout the United States, Europe, and the Middle East and his work has been published in major architecture publications in the United States, England, and Germany. In 1976, he began work for Philip Johnson/ John Burgee and, with Random House, produced the book, *Johnson/ Burgee Architecture.*

ULI
ROSE

Born in Germany, he learned a lot, he said, from his father and grandfather, both of whom were photographers. He went to Paris and started in fashion photography, then came to New York City in 1976 to work for *The New York Times Magazine* and other publications.

He lives with his wife and two children on the thirty-fourth-floor of a high-rise with a panoramic view of the fifty-ninth Street and Triborough bridges. The airy apartment is sparsely furnished with white wicker and lots of plants and paintings.

MARK
ROSS

Born in New York City, Mr. Ross was educated at the Art Students League, the People's Art Center (the Museum of Modern Art), what is now Carnegie-Mellon University, and the School of Visual Arts.

His work has been published in many major design and general publications.

"Interior photography is still in its fledgling years," he said, "and now is the time to progress it toward something special, something other than documentation. Photography for me, and this includes my personal work as well, is a joy, and I believe that is what enables me to bring all that I have to it. Bringing all is a prime requisite."

DEIDI
VON SCHAEWEN

Born in Berlin in 1944, Ms. Von Schaewen has lived in Barcelona and New York City and now lives in Paris. She began taking pictures about twenty years ago, and has published a book on the subject that inspired her first photographs, *Walls,* on exterior walls. Besides taking photographs, she is a graphic designer and makes films.

She would like to live in a loft, having lived in one in New York, but they are hard to find in Paris, so she is waiting her turn. "The bigger and emptier the space the better." Architecture, she feels, has become one of the most important professions because of the power it has to create or destroy an environment.

MARINA
SCHINZ

Born in Zurich, Switzerland, she took advertising pictures at the age of eleven with her first camera, a Brownie, but lacked the courage to market them. She was headed for an academic career but was intercepted by New York City and photography.

She and her husband, art gallery president Larry

Rubin, spend winter workdays in their Manhattan apartment overlooking Central Park, but during the warmer months and on weekends, they retire to their twenty-five-acre farm of apple trees, horses, and a spare, simple house filled with flowers, art, children, dogs, and Ms. Schinz' own fabric designs.

JOE
STANDART

While studying for a degree in history at Williams College, Mr. Standart participated in a program that took him to four regions of the country, and during that time he developed his interest in photography. He subsequently spent several summers photographing remote regions of Alaska for the National Parks Services.

Since 1977 he has had a studio in New York from which he has done a variety of commercial assignments for major publications.

He plans to move soon to larger quarters and is particularly interested in pursuing projects incorporating the concepts of photographing both people and environments.

GEORGE WHITE

CHRISTIAN STAUB

Christian Staub was born in Switzerland. In 1938, he traveled to Paris and began to paint. A year later, he began photographing with a pin-hole camera bought at a flea market. He went to Zurich in 1940, on the day before the Occupation, to study photography. His work has since been published in many Swiss and Austrian magazines.

He has taught cinematography and photography in Switzerland and India and at the University of California at Berkeley. In 1967 he moved to America to teach photography in the Department of Architecture at the University of Washington in Seattle.

GENE MAGGIO/THE NEW YORK TIMES

JAY STEFFY

A native of Los Angeles and the son of a Hollywood filmmaker, Jay Steffy began designing interiors in the mid-sixties and stopped in the late 1970s. His interiors were known for their unusual approach to living space and atmosphere.

His photographing of interiors began with his recording of his own designs.

Then he branched out to photographing other designers' work.

He lives in California.

CARL E. GUTTENBERGER

PETER VITALE

Peter Vitale was born a triplet, one of three boys. A heavy load, he said, for his parents, who already had one son. Due partially to this, he believes, his parents moved back to their native Italy several months after the birth of the triplets. They stayed for several years, and, he said, his orientation toward language and culture was originally Italian.

His post-Italian schooling was all in the New York area. He rceived his degree at Queens College, New York, where he majored in art studio. Essentially, he said, he was intent on being a painter, but things worked out even better with photography. "I am still painting," he said, "only with light instead of a brush."

STEVE ERLE

BARBRA WALZ

The work of photographer Barbra Walz has appeared in many publications. Her book, *The Fashion Makers,* is a look at the lives of the top American fashion designers in their home environments. Based in New York City, she has traveled extensively photographing the life-styles of personalities.

"It is my job," she said, "as a photographer of personalities to capture in a series or sometimes in one photograph the essence of that person and their life-style. This whole process, from meeting the person, my involvement with them, the shooting itself, and having others enjoy the published work has become my life-style and one which I love."

Camera Shy

PAUL
WARCHOL

Born in New Jersey in 1954, he received his Bachelor of Fine Arts from the Cooper Union in 1976. He began photographing architecture in 1976. While compiling a project on highway architecture, he met Ezra Stoller and later became his assistant. He joined Esto Photographics in 1978.

He lives on one floor of a brownstone in Brooklyn with his wife, some furniture designed by Alvar Aalto, the Scandinavian designer, a Japanese tonsu, and "some hand-me-down stuff I want to get rid of." He also has a coffee table, upon which, he said, this book will take up permanent residence.

He loves to travel and he is taking flying lessons.

And also

JEAN-PASCAL
BILLAUD

GAYLEN
MOORE